JOBS
AND GENDER

JOBS AND GENDER

A Study of Occupational Prestige

Christine E. Bose

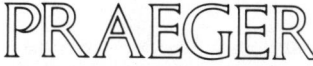

PRAEGER SPECIAL STUDIES • PRAEGER SCIENTIFIC

New York • Philadelphia • Eastbourne, UK
Toronto • Hong Kong • Tokyo • Sydney

Library of Congress Cataloging in Publication Data

Bose, Christine E.
    Jobs and gender.

    Bibliography: p.
    Includes index.
    1. Women--Employment--United States.
2. Occupational prestige--United States. I. Title.
HD6058.B67 1985   305.4'3'00973   85-6305
ISBN 0-03-071692-6 (alk. paper)

Published in 1985 by Praeger Publishers
CBS Educational and Professional Publishing, a Division of CBS Inc.
521 Fifth Avenue, New York, NY 10175 USA

© 1985 by Praeger Publishers

All rights reserved

56789 052 987654321

Printed in the United States of America on acid-free paper

INTERNATIONAL OFFICES

Orders from outside the United States should be sent to the appropriate address listed below. Orders from areas not listed below should be placed through CBS International Publishing, 383 Madison Ave., New York, NY 10175 USA

Australia, New Zealand
Holt Saunders, Pty, Ltd., 9 Waltham St., Artarmon, N.S.W. 2064, Sydney, Australia

Canada
Holt, Rinehart & Winston of Canada, 55 Horner Ave., Toronto, Ontario, Canada M8Z 4X6

Europe, the Middle East, & Africa
Holt Saunders, Ltd., 1 St. Anne's Road, Eastbourne, East Sussex, England BN21 3UN

Japan
Holt Saunders, Ltd., Ichibancho Central Building, 22-1 Ichibancho, 3rd Floor, Chiyodaku, Tokyo, Japan

Hong Kong, Southeast Asia
Holt Saunders Asia, Ltd., 10 Fl, Intercontinental Plaza, 94 Granville Road, Tsim Sha Tsui East, Kowloon, Hong Kong

Manuscript submissions should be sent to the Editorial Director, Praeger Publishers, 521 Fifth Avenue, New York, NY 10175 USA

To Edna, Arthur, and Edna

PREFACE

In the study of social mobility or status attainment, people are frequently classified according to the occupations they hold. Since the mid-1960s, prestige has been among the predominant continuous scale measures of occupational position. However, until the publication in limited edition of my monograph <u>Jobs and Gender: Sex and Occupational Prestige</u> in 1973, no thorough analysis of the impact of gender on occupational prestige had been carried out. That study was frequently cited, and I often received requests for further information on the scores that were developed.

Since that time, others have done research on the interaction of gender with prestige, but this study remains the only one to simultaneously and systematically investigate the prestige of a wide range of gender-typed jobs, controlling for the effects of gender incumbency and rater characteristics and using a representative population sample of respondents.

Prestige scores have been the basis of the frequently used Duncan socioeconomic index (SEI). However, that scale does not adequately take into account the interactions of gender, prestige, income, and education. Therefore, this new book takes the earlier monograph a step further by constructing separate socioeconomic scores for women and men, called the "Bose Index" by the National Longitudinal Surveys. Chapter 5 examines the derivation of these scores and their relationship to previous Duncan SEI and National Opinion Research Center indexes. Appendix E presents the actual separate incumbent Bose scores for the 1960, 1970, and 1980 detailed census occupations and should prove of great use to mobility researchers.

Chapter 1 provides a review of the most recent literature on gender and social standing, which will be of interest to researchers and students alike.

Chapter 3 details a new model that estimates the ways in which incumbent prestige scores given to occupational titles vary from the no-incumbent scores as a function of characteristics of the respondents, the occupations involved, and the nature of the experimental treatments. Psychologists and vocational guidance professionals, as well as researchers on stratification, will be concerned with the implications of the resulting attitudes revealed toward employed women and men.

Women's studies researchers will be concerned with the effects of occupational segregation on social standing, as well as with the analysis in Chapter 4, which focuses on the major non-labor force occupation of housewife/househusband. Here the prestige of nonpaying roles is examined, and a prestige score suitable for status attainment studies is derived. Housewife is compared with other gender-stereotyped work, with its labor force equivalents, and with other nonpaying roles.

Since prestige is based on consensus over the reputed social standing of occupations, Chapter 6 explores both the degree of agreement among respondents and the degree of variation in the ratings of particular occupations. Considerable consensus is found.

Chapter 7 summarizes the findings on jobs and gender. Although the achieved aspect of occupation is more important than the ascribed characteristic of gender in the determination of incumbent prestige, gender does significantly impact occupational prestige. This chapter indicates the ways in which gender will continue to interact with occupational prestige, and points to those effects that can be expected to decline over time.

The monograph concludes that gender effects which are attitudinal will change more rapidly than those which reflect the structural problem of occupational segregation.

ACKNOWLEDGMENTS

My research on gender and occupational prestige began in Baltimore, Maryland, and has continued to follow me back and forth across the continental United States, involving many people who deserve appreciation. With each geographic move as well as with the concomitant changes in the foci of the women's movement, my thoughts on the relationships between gender and class stratification have clarified.

From the beginning of this project, Peter H. Rossi, my dissertation advisor and friend, was supportive of my ideas and never tried to stop me from pursuing the fascinating avenues of non-labor force prestige as well as the more usual ones. At the same time, a research and development grant (number 91-24-72-44) from the U.S. Department of Labor, Manpower Administration, facilitated the actual data gathering and the early stages of data analysis. Mary Lee Considine and Ruby Creighton of Sidney Hollander and Associates, a commercial survey firm in Baltimore, did excellent work shepherding the household survey in and out of the field without the loss of a single vignette. And my friends in the Great Atlantic Radio Conspiracy always prevented me from losing sight of the forest for the closeness of the trees.

While living in Seattle, I became self-taught in the then new field of women's studies, and the Women Studies Program at the University of Washington deserves thanks for the support it gave me in helping further develop my ideas.

With my return to the northeast, I have been able to pull together all of my materials on gendered prestige into written form. This has been facilitated by the intellectual support of the Women and Work Research Group, of which I am a member, as well as through my membership in the feminist scholars group, MF1. At the State University of New York at Albany, my colleagues in both the Women's Studies Program and the Sociology Department have encouraged my endeavors, while Debbie Steiger and Eileen Crary provided excellent typing of my extensive tables.

Particular thanks must go to Edna Acosta-Belén, without whose support this book could never have been completed. She encouraged me to revise and expand the original monograph, <u>Jobs and Gender: Sex and Occupational Prestige</u>, published by the Center for Metropolitan Planning and Research at The Johns Hopkins University in 1973. Her belief in my work and her patience with my long days and nights at the computer provided the needed family support that spouses, children, or cats most frequently provide to others.

Some of the material in this volume has appeared in various forms at previous times. The author gratefully acknowledges the contributions of Peter H. Rossi as coauthor of the article "Gender and Jobs: Prestige Standings of Occupations as Affected by Gender" [American Sociological Review, 1983, Vol. 48 (June):316-30] of which Chapter 3 is an edited version.

CONTENTS

PREFACE	vii
ACKNOWLEDGMENTS	ix
LIST OF TABLES	xiv

Chapter

1   CRITICAL OVERVIEW OF GENDER AND
      OCCUPATIONAL PRESTIGE   1

Gender and Social Standing	1
Gender and Prestige Literature	4
Gendered Prestige	4
Incumbents and Raters	6
Stereotyped Jobs	8
The Homemaker	10
Other Job Characteristics	13
Conclusion	14

2   RESEARCH STRATEGY   15

The Occupational Sample	15
The Measurement of Gender	17
The Experimental Treatments	18
The Respondent Sample: Householders	19
The Respondent Sample: College Students	20
The Questionnaire and Rating Task	21
Mode of Analysis	23

3   PRESTIGE AND GENDER: THE INCUMBENT,
      THE USUAL INCUMBENT, AND THE RESPONDENT   27

Incumbent Gender Effects	31
Sex Segregation: Status of Women's and Men's Jobs	34
Gender and the Judger	37
Conclusion	41

4	SAME ROLE, DIFFERENT PRESTIGE: THE HOUSEWIFE AND THE HOUSEHUSBAND	44
	The Status of Homemaking	45
	Status Equivalents of the Homemaker Role	46
	Status Alternatives to the Homemaker Role	49
	Effects of Respondent Characteristics	52
	Conclusion	56
5	THE RELATIONSHIP OF INCOME, EDUCATION, AND PRESTIGE: THE BOSE INDEX AND DUNCAN SCORES	58
	The Relationship Between National Opinion Research Center and No Incumbent Scores	58
	The Relationship Between Duncan and No Incumbent Scores	60
	The Bose Index	64
	Prestige, Income, and Education in Gender-Segregated Jobs	67
	Male-Based Equations and Female Incumbent Scores	68
	Conclusion	70
6	CONSENSUS AMONG INDIVIDUALS AND IN OCCUPATIONAL RATINGS	72
	Individual's Consensus with the Group	73
	Variation in Consensus on Occupations	79
	Conclusion	88
7	SUMMARY AND CONCLUSIONS: GENDER AND JOBS	89
	Summary	90
	Discussion	98

Appendix

A	THE QUESTIONNAIRES	101
	Household Questionnaire	101
	College Questionnaire	117
B	THE OCCUPATIONAL SAMPLE AND SAMPLING METHOD	127

C   COMPARISON OF DUNCAN SOCIOECONOMIC INDEX,
    NATIONAL OPINION RESEARCH CENTER (SIEGEL),
    AND BOSE NO INCUMBENT SCORES   139

D   PRESTIGE SCORES FOR THE ORIGINAL 110 JOBS,
    BY TREATMENT AND SAMPLE   144

E   BOSE INDEX FOR CENSUS OCCUPATIONS: 1960,
    1970, AND 1980 CENSUSES   151

    1960 Bose Index   151
    1970 Bose Index   166
    1980 Bose Index   179

BIBLIOGRAPHY   195

INDEX   203

ABOUT THE AUTHOR   207

LIST OF TABLES

Table

3-1	Regression of Prestige Ratings on Occupation, Treatment, and Respondent Characteristics	29
3-2	Prestige Scores (from Control Treatment) for Jobs with High and Low Percentages of Women Jobholders	36
3-3	Regressions of Prestige Ratings on Respondent and Other Experimental Characteristics by Respondent Gender for Each Sample	38
3-4	Regressions of Prestige Ratings on Respondent and Other Experimental Characteristics by Household Prestige for Each Sample	40
4-1	Average Status of No Incumbent Jobs Roughly Approximating Duties of a Homemaker	48
4-2	Women's Occupations with No Incumbent Prestige Higher Than Housewife or 51 Points (Household Sample)	50
4-3	Regression of Housewife Rating on Respondent Characteristics (Household Sample)	54
5-1	Correlations Among Median Income, Median Years of Education, and Prestige of Job by Gender of Incumbent (Household Sample)	62
6-1	Average Correlations of Individual Ratings with Treatment Means (by Sample)	74
6-2	Regression of Individual R^2 Values on Selected Individual Characteristics (Household Sample)	76
6-3	Regression of Individual R^2 Values on Selected Individual Characteristics (College Sample)	78
6-4	Standard Deviations for Mean Occupational Prestige Ratings of Household Sample (by Incumbent's Gender)	80

1

CRITICAL OVERVIEW OF GENDER AND OCCUPATIONAL PRESTIGE

GENDER AND SOCIAL STANDING

The increasing numbers of women entering the paid labor force in the United States since the 1950s have raised several issues concerning conventional measures of social standing, including both prestige and socioeconomic status scores. While theoretical inquiry on the basis and nature of women's social position could have begun earlier, pragmatic concerns with the contributions of working women and the women's movement itself brought such questions to the fore in the late 1960s and early 1970s. The most obvious issue was the inappropriateness of using husband's occupation as the sole indicator of family social standing in two-earner households. Several studies have since shown that wives' jobs do affect their families' social standing (Rossi et al., 1974; Ritter and Hargens, 1975; Nock and Rossi, 1978). Interest also developed in the occupational mobility of women as individuals. Therefore, the almost exclusive attention of past studies (Hodge et al., 1965) on the social standing of predominantly male occupations, where women's jobs were included only in a nonsystematic manner, was no longer justified. Further, it was no longer clear if, within particular occupations, women's occupational standing was the same as that of male incumbents (Havens and Tully, 1972) or if the social standing of any occupation was affected by its gender composition.

While these issues have been debated separately, no study simultaneously and systematically investigated the social standing of a wide range of gender-typed jobs, controlling for the effects of gender incumbency and rater characteristics and using a representative population sample, as does the research reported here. [For an earlier version of the analysis, see Bose (1973).] Prestige scores were chosen for this project because they have been used extensively in their own right and have formed the basis for the Duncan socioeconomic index (SEI) (Blau and Duncan, 1967). Although prestige is a subjective measure based on repute of position, and SEI is more directly based on income and education components of occupational status, these conceptual differences have not prevented both scores from being used in mobility studies with only minor differences in findings. The lack of difference in results found using the two scales may be attributed to several features. First, Siegel prestige scores (Siegel, 1971) and Duncan SEI scores are highly intercorrelated. Second, both measures have been shown to be strongly and positively correlated with occupational complexity and clerical ability, while being more moderately related to other occupational dimensions such as social relations and even negatively associated with unpleasant working conditions and heavy physical activity (Parcel and Mueller, 1983). Some differences in intergenerational mobility have been found (Treas and Tyree, 1979) when comparing the Duncan SEI and the Treiman international prestige scales (Treiman, 1977) for father/son and father/daughter mobility, but neither scale had been modified at that point to measure appropriately status for female incumbents.

More recently, rigorous attempts have been made, particularly by Stevens and Featherman (1981), to include women as incumbents in the construction of Duncan SEI-type indexes. Similar efforts have been made by Powers and Holmberg (1982) to update the comparable Nam and Powers index (Nam and Powers, 1965). Stevens and Featherman point out that such revisions are necessary not only because the original scales were derived from data solely on men, but because the relationship of education and income to job status has changed since 1950, because prestige can be better measured than Duncan was originally able to do, and because improved measures of education and income are now possible. As a result, they develop two contemporary versions of the Duncan SEI, one based on the attributes of the 1970 male labor force and one based on those of the total labor force.

Powers and Holmberg (1982) point to the importance of using total labor force data, and their analysis indicates the resulting changes among specific detailed occupations and for major occupational groups. Whereas the top categories (professional, technical, and managers and administrators) and the bottom-ranked (farmers and farm managers, service workers, laborers, farm laborers, and private household workers) occupational groupings remain the same whether using male or total labor force data, differences in the relative positions of sales, clerical, and craft work occur when using scores based on the total labor force. Using male data, the ordering is sales (66), clerical (56), and then craft (49); but using total labor force data, sales and craft (55) fall above clerical (51). The inclusion of women, who are concentrated in the lower ranks of both clerical and sales work, decreases the status of these roles. Thus, including data on women causes a switch in the relative status of craft and clerical work. Powers and Holmberg therefore argue for the usage of total labor force data, which more accurately reflect the different patterns of occupational concentration by gender and the differing education and income attainment of women and men.

In a review of both prestige and socioeconomic status indexes, Boyd and McRoberts (1982) concur on the need to move away from male-only data. They indicate that women have a lower average socioeconomic status than men either when measures are calculated from the total labor force or when female status is calculated from the characteristics of women and then compared with male SEI scores calculated from the characteristics of men. (When SEI scores based on male-only data are used, women appear to have a higher socioeconomic status than do men.) In fact, since an SEI based on the total labor force does not explicitly take into account a gender-specific occupational hierarchy, Boyd and McRoberts indicate that two separate indexes could be desirable. When status attainment is examined in this way, using male-derived Blishen-Roberts scores for men and female-derived Blishen-Carroll scores for women, gender differences in the attainment process are sharper than those obtained under the assumption of a single socioeconomic hierarchy. Thus, these authors take the index development process one step further by suggesting that an SEI based on the total labor force will not sufficiently take into account the gender-specific occupational hierarchy. Our study follows this directive by developing separate prestige scores for men and women.

These new prestige scores should facilitate the study of career and intergenerational mobility for women. First, previous research could only estimate scores for women's jobs based on the known relationship of average (usually male) incumbent income and education to prestige, whereas our measures are specific to the kinds of occupations held by women. Many of the early National Opinion Research Center (NORC) scores given to census titles are composite measures of several specific titles of male incumbent-dominated jobs. Most of the female gender-dominated jobs included in this study have never before been directly rated by respondent samples. Moreover, because these jobs are rated with female incumbents, more accurate prestige projections can be made for all women, based on the known income and education contributions of women incumbents to their prestige. Second, the debate of the early 1970s concerning the "amount" of social mobility experienced by women as compared to men (DeJong et al., 1971; Tyree and Treas, 1974; Treiman and Terrell, 1975; Featherman and Hauser, 1976; McClendon, 1976) illustrated uncertainty as to whether or not the measures of occupational attainment used are equally valid for male and female incumbents, especially in gender-stereotyped jobs. This research answers that question for prestige. Third, studies of career mobility of women have had problems handling occupational "gaps."* Using the data base here, a prestige score for housewives is provided, making possible comparisons of that role with others.

GENDER AND PRESTIGE LITERATURE

Discussions of gender and occupational prestige have focused mainly on three concerns: whether women and men incumbents in the same occupational slot receive the same levels of prestige, especially in sex-stereotyped jobs; the prestige of predominantly female and predominantly male occupations; and the correlates of occupational prestige, assessing in particular whether or not income and education contribute to prestige among women in the same way as among men. Two relatively new issues are the prestige of the housewife and the effect of rater characteristics, with stress on gender differentials. These issues are discussed further below, preceded by background information on the general subject of gendered prestige.

Gendered Prestige

Prestige is the repute an individual gains by holding social positions. There are many possible roles an individual can hold at one time, and it is not clear which of these is the most salient in determining prestige. The important variable could be occupation, education, income, ethnicity, race, gender, age, or life-style, to name only a few. In general, prestige reflects capitalist and patriarchal ideology about what is important to society.

The premise of this research is that occupation is the major contributor to social status, and especially to prestige. Most of the arguments in favor of occupational importance stress one of two factors. The first is visibility: Most people know what others do for

---

*Interestingly enough, mobility researchers were able early to solve the problem of how to handle periods of military service for men, which is a comparable issue.

a living, even if they do not know the income of their neighbors. Second, occupation is important as it reflects the relationship of an individual to the means of production and thus determines income, and therefore life-style, as well as power, irrespective of visibility.

Many stratification theorists also conclude that occupation is important in determining social status. For example, both Parsons (1954) and Warner et al. (1949) discussed social standing as determined by the consensus of persons on the existence of a hierarchical ranking. Other authors as diverse as Marx (1966), Weber (1946), and Davis and Moore (1945) discussed the importance of occupation in determining social standing, regardless of whether this dimension is perceived by members of society.

Although the intersection of gender and occupational stratification is important for feminist theorists, most sociologists do not discuss the effect on the total stratification system when occupations are assigned to women. Gender is assumed to have no effect on occupational prestige, and men are implicitly thought of as jobholders, as well as the individuals who define household status. These assumptions reflect a sexist ideology. The purpose of this research is to test the validity of such assumptions and rectify the prestige scores in current usage where necessary.

We take the position that conceptually our new ratings are those of occupational prestige modified by the sex of the incumbent, and not those of gender prestige and occupational prestige combined to form a new social standing variable. "Pure" occupational prestige has never been studied because it is inherently confounded with the sex of the incumbent as implied by the percentage of women (or men) in any given occupation. An occupation involves a constellation of subcharacteristics such as gender, race, and age of the typical incumbent, a presumed income, an average education usually required, and a sense of the importance of the job to the current society. While deference to superiors may not be implied in the global measurement of prestige, respondents are surely seeing occupations as better or worse in a hierarchy of socioeconomic factors. This is what leads authors [such as Goldthorpe and Hope (1972)] to suggest that prestige is an evaluative judgment, the measurement of which will vary with objective attributes of an occupation, such as rewards, qualifications, tasks, and work environment. All of these contextual characteristics contribute to an occupation's prestige. However, our methodology allows the separation of various gender affects (rater, actual incumbent, and usual incumbent) from other aspects of prestige.

These new prestige ratings are subjective measures of status because they are the results of collective judgments as to the standing of jobs. They are not objective ratings, made on the basis of a fixed, although not necessarily popularly perceived, relationship to a known criterion such as income or wealth. As a result, there is more variance in our ratings of perceived status than there would be under the latter conditions.

Incumbents and Raters

The literature on men and women in the same job follows two tracks: First, there are studies that compare the mean occupational statuses of men and women incumbents. In a comprehensive review of the stratification literature based on research by Bose (1973) and others, Acker (1980) concludes that traditional women's jobs have a lower average status than male-dominated jobs; but since few women are to be found in extremely low-prestige occupations, the equal average status of all working women and men obscures this fact.

Related work by Powell and Jacobs (1983) compares the variation in ranking of women and men in occupations. Their evidence, drawn from a college group among which one might expect more consensus than from a random population sample, indicates that there is less agreement regarding female incumbents in occupations than for either nongendered prestige or for male jobholders. This lower level of consensus is found among all occupations, not only for women in nontraditional jobs, but for those in gender-stereotyped ones as well. Further, this disagreement is found among women and among men as respondents, and is not simply the result of women disagreeing with men on how female incumbents should be rated. Powell and Jacobs interpret their results as indicating that the level of social regard for women's labor force roles is still in flux, and advise caution in attributing either SEI or prestige scores to women's labor force roles. These findings are provocative, and therefore this volume explores the relative consensus for men and women when they are rated by a population versus a college sample and over a wider range of jobs than were included in the study of Powell and Jacobs.

Second, there are studies that explicitly examine the status of women and men as incumbents in the same job. Early work in this area was done within the personnel and guidance field by Stefflre et al. (1968) and Hicks (1969). These studies were based on small samples of occupations and yielded conflicting findings. Stefflre and coauthors used a list of 20 occupations chosen in no particular systematic manner, but so that the jobs presented to respondents could be held by members of either gender. The respondents were women and men in the spring and fall sections of a pupil personnel services course. They were shown a picture of a normal curve that had the numbers 1 (low) through 9 (high) printed below it, indicating that 5 was to be the mean score. Students were asked to place the letter corresponding to each job next to a number on the curve. Four separate forms were used: one with all male incumbents, one with all female incumbents, and two others with male and female incumbents in alternating patterns (one form began with a male incumbent and the other with a female incumbent).

The data were analyzed using a one-way analysis of variance for each of three variables: gender of incumbent, gender of respondent, and treatment as homogeneous or mixed. The authors found few differences on these variables across all of the jobs, and those that did occur in the fall sample were not replicated in the spring. Stefflre et al. continued to maintain that there should be differences according to the gender of the incumbent and suggested either instrument failure or problems with the particular respondents who may have been socialized not to make differentiating judgments.

However, there seem to be other failings in the research design. First, the insistence on a mean of 5 in each treatment would obscure any difference in the overall distribution of women versus men incumbents. Second, it was not possible to test for the pure effect of an incumbent, and the addition of a treatment with no person attached could have been useful. Third, the occupational sample excluded gender-stereotyped jobs, eliminating the possibility that ranking differences occur primarily within or between such stereotyped roles. Finally, the method of analysis, which focused on the individual job, ignored overall structural effects.

A related study was carried out a year later by Hicks (1969) who attempted to chastise Stefflre et al. for finding no differences in the ratings of male and female incumbents. Using a sample of 1,100 secondary school children in Zambia, half of whom were male and half female, Hicks had 32 occupations rated for their prestige on a scale of 1 (high) to 5 (low). For the three occupations of doctor, lawyer, and teacher, respondents were asked if a male or a female incumbent would generally be more highly regarded. Female incumbents were uniformly rated lower than male incumbents by respondents of both genders, but girls rated the female incumbents slightly higher than did the boys. The former is attributed to patterns of male dominance in Africa, whereas the author suggested the latter effect was due to women rating their own occupations higher than would others. However, the research cited in support of this statement implies that accessibility to the job is an important factor, and we suspect that the occupations of doctor or lawyer were no more open to women in Zambia than they were in the United States at the time.

Several obvious critiques of these works are visible. First, the rationale for selecting the three occupations is not clear, nor is the relative position of women and men in the Zambian work force presented. Second, the jobs all appear to be high-prestige ones, so that the effects may be caused by the level of respect accorded to the jobs. Finally, we do not know how much lower women were rated than were men: Measurement was calculated in terms of more, less, or the same regard as a man would obtain. Thus, a difference may have existed, but may not have been statistically significant.

More recent work by Bose (1973), Nilson (1976), and Powell and Jacobs (1984) appears of greater generality. Nilson's study, innovative in having male, female, and married female incumbents rated within each job, had the major drawback of focusing on ratings of a small haphazard sample of 17 jobs. Powell and Jacobs's study, using more occupations (50), was also limited, since their only respondents were young students and the occupations were not selected for representativeness. Both Nilson and Powell and Jacobs focused on the differences found in clearly sex-stereotyped occupations (that is, occupations usually identified as held predominantly by one gender). Powell and Jacobs's results are of special interest because they found prestige differences according to gender of the raters, with men giving markedly different prestige ratings (judged by correlations) to female incumbent than to male and no incumbent jobs, and with women not distinguishing female incumbent prestige from the general no incumbent prestige hierarchy. Bose's research combines the advantages of both other studies by using a broad range of occupations and a stratified household sample, while rating female, male, and no incumbent jobs.

Stereotyped Jobs

Clara Menger (1932) conducted the earliest research on women's jobs. She had a sample of male and female students rank "thirty-five occupations in which girls and women find employment," using methods similar to those of George Counts (1925) who had conducted the first empirical prestige studies in order to find the relative social placement of the teaching profession. Menger reported a social hierarchy of occupations for women, with physician at the top and scrubwoman at the bottom. The eight jobs that appeared in both Counts's and Menger's sample were ranked in the same order, but the precise relationship between the prestige of women's and men's jobs is not detailed. The sex of the job incumbent was implied by the research technique to be female, so we cannot determine if the rankings would have been similar with male incumbents.

In 1940 Raymond Stevens had 150 college women rank 25 occupations that women go into according to their financial return, contribution to society, prestige, and personal first choice. There were no substantially new findings except that social class of respondent had no effect upon the rankings. Again, there was no systematic choice of jobs used as stimuli, the incumbents were assumed to be female, and, in addition, all of the respondents were female. This study was followed by Baudler and Paterson's (1948) research on 29 women's occupations. Using Counts's method they found a rank order correlation of .98 between ratings of female and male respondents.

More recent research on the impact of proportions of women usually in a job on its prestige provides conflicting results and interpretations. For example, Kolstad (1977) found that "pink-collar" jobs are more highly evaluated than their earnings and ability requirements appear to justify. He concluded that the proportion of women in a position elevates its prestige standing compared to its earnings, reasoning that such jobs are better than their main alternative, housework. Of course, these findings are subject to an alternative explanation, namely, that women are discriminated against and are being paid less than is ordinarily warranted by the prestige of their jobs.

England (1979), on the other hand, found that the percentage of women in an occupation makes no significant contribution to prestige, and that jobs have the prestige one would predict based on their complexity and training. She argued that it is only in the most prestigeful top 5 percent of all jobs that women are underrepresented. Otherwise the distribution of women in the prestige hierarchy is similar to that of men.

Resolving the seeming conflict with the findings of Kolstad, England argued that prestige standings act quite differently from income and education levels. She summarized previous research by citing the several researchers (Siegel, 1971; Stevenson, 1975; Treiman and Terrell, 1975; England and McLaughlin, 1979) who found that predominantly female occupations have lower average salaries than one would predict based upon their prestige. This finding was elaborated by McLaughlin (1978), who concluded that the task composition of men's and women's jobs is different at the same level of prestige. These task differences are a partial cause of the income differences, although sex identification of the occupation also has an impact on earnings, independent of prestige and nature of job task.

Both England (1979) and McLaughlin (1978) concluded that prestige does not serve as an indicator of equivalent occupations when used in income attainment research comparing male- and female-dominated jobs. They favored indicators describing the nature of the task. While concurring with these findings, this volume also asks a different question: Are female and male incumbents' prestige equivalent when in the same sex-identified job? This question remains one of importance for individual-level social standing studies.

The Homemaker

It is still often assumed that the status of the housewife comes solely from her husband's job (Glenn et al., 1974), instead of obtaining an independent measurement of the status of homemakers. Authors forget that other kinds of power bases—stocks and bonds, political position, personal strength, or non-labor force work—contribute to social standing. So it is with the millions of U.S. housewives and thousands of male homemakers whose contributions to the economy at large are often forgotten, never counted in the gross national product, and until recently rarely considered in studies of women's, let alone men's, occupational prestige. Frequently, their status is mentioned, but then ignored, because of the perceived measurement difficulties.

Several researchers have examined the role attributes to the housewife, yet there is still much disagreement on how people view the housewife role. Many students feel the role of housewife is no longer a viable economic role, and perhaps not even a legitimate social role. Helena Lopata (1971, pp. 139-40) found that women see the role as "just a housewife" and defined the position thus:

> In addition, the role is not easily located in the occupational social structure. Most Americans are not even sure whether it belongs there: it lacks the basic criteria of most jobs. It has no organized social circle which judges performance and has the right to fire for incompetence, no specific pay scale, and no measurement against other performers of the same role or against circle members. It is vague, open to any woman who gets married, regardless of ability; it has no union and belongs to no organizational structure.
> On the other hand, what kind of role could it be, if not an occupational one? All family roles are located within a kinship organization, but it clearly has no place on a family tree. . . . The counterpart male role is always a specific occupation.

A CRITICAL OVERVIEW

This state of affairs results in the role's devaluation, conflict with other roles, and psychological strain for the performers. One of its major problems is its lack of high social rank in any ranking system. As an economic role, it is immediately placed low in that status hierarchy, because of a lack of wage or salary scale. As an occupational role, it lacks many traits of the more prestigious jobs. As a family role it seems merely an adjunct to the more important sets of relations of wife and mother.

On the other hand, Mirra Komarovsky (1962, p. 49) found that blue-collar women's attitudes toward the role were not so negative:

> We find little evidence of status frustrations among working class wives. They accept housewifery. There is hardly a trace in the interviews of the low prestige educated housewives sometimes attach to their role. . . . This is not to say that [working class] women are all satisfied homemakers. But their discontent is not caused by the low evaluation they place upon domesticity, stemming rather from other frustrations of housewifery.

Ferree (1976) agreed with Komarovsky that working-class housewives were somewhat happier than middle-class housewives, but disagreed with the thesis that working-class women preferred housework to paid work. She found that fulltime housewives were more dissatisfied with the way they were spending their lives than either part- or fulltime employed wives. Low self-esteem was associated with housework, and the role was found to be socially isolating and powerless. Vanek's conclusions (1976) were compatible with these results. She found that most wives were satisfied with housework, but that the satisfaction of those with waged jobs was higher than that of those doing fulltime housework.

However, in terms of status, Ann Oakley (1974, pp. 70-78) concluded that both working- and middle-class wives generally perceive the housewife's standing to be low. This class convergence was also suggested by Vanek (1978), who felt the limited existing data indicated that housewives' perceptions of their work were concurring and that status differences in homemaker role content were narrowing. The theory was also implicit in Glazer's work (1976), which concluded that the primarily social service role of housewife defined women's caste status.

Each of the previous studies gave some sense of what the homemaker's standing might be, but none of them provided concrete measures of the role's prestige. Housewife status was first rated when Menger (1932) had a sample of students rank 35 jobs in which women were usually employed. Homemaker ranked at sixteenth place, but there was considerable disagreement as to its status, since men rated it highly and women rated it rather low. These results caused considerable distress to the author, who worried that women did not seem to have the appropriate regard for their probable future careers. While this average ranking foreshadowed our findings, no author compared housewife with a random sample of occupations. More recently, Arnott and Bengtson (1970) found faculty wives ranked homemaker in the middle of 20 job options. Similarly, Eichler (1976) found housewife was ranked fifty-second of 93 randomly selected jobs by 180 randomly selected respondents.

In a study similar to the one described here, Nilson (1978) used only 17 occupations with treatments similar to Bose's female-only and male-only incumbent formats (1973) to rate housewife as well as other occupations. In her all female incumbent treatment, Nilson found the housewife prestige score to be a rather high 70 points. Therefore, much of her analysis was devoted to disaggregating rater characteristics that explained variation around the housewife score. Innovatively, Nilson also had respondents rate the general social standing of seven diverse housewives, each of whom was presented as being married to a man in a different occupation. She found that husband's occupation influenced wife's prestige, and that controlling on husband's occupation reduced the variance in housewife prestige.

Recent research (Dworkin, 1981) in the Duncan-Reiss SEI tradition (Reiss, 1961) has assessed the status of the housewife to be similar to that of the prestige for the role derived by Bose (1980) and expanded upon herein. Dworkin's research is based on 501 female respondents who compared the role of housewife with each of 20 occupations selected at 2 per decile from the 1961 Duncan-Reiss index. Subjects performed paired comparisons of housewife with each of the other jobs, determining whether housewife was higher, lower, or equal in status. The resulting scores for housewife were distributed normally with a mean at the fifth decile. Although Dworkin's study was limited to female subjects and was based on SEI measures, it does provide corroboration for the results of our study. Both studies find variation in housewife's rating according to the social standing of the respondent, but our study also finds variation by gender of respondent—a conclusion not possible from Dworkin's data.

On the whole, social mobility studies require more information about the prestige of the housewife than has thus far been available. A single prestige score for the homemaker based on a random sample of respondents, knowledge of how it compares with other roles, and background on the variation in attitude toward it by social subgroups are essential. The research described here provides such information, as well as a comparison with the neglected role of househusband.

Other Job Characteristics

Parcel and Mueller (1983) have innovatively determined the several ways in which occupations may be differentiated according to the skills required of incumbents and the characteristics of the work tasks the incumbents perform, and compared these dimensions with the status dimensions provided by both prestige and socioeconomic scores. Using occupational characteristics derived from the Dictionary of Occupational Titles (1965 edition), which were aggregated and weighted to match the three-digit occupational 1970 U.S. Census codes, they perform a factor analysis that results in seven interpretable substantive dimensions of jobs. These elements are job complexity, interpersonal relations or interaction with people and things, required physical activities, physical dexterity and perceptual abilities, unpredictability or frequent change of job duties, clerical aptitude, and unpleasantness of work activities.

Further analysis reveals that complexity is a vertical dimension of occupational differentiation, whereas people-things, physical activity, physical dexterity, unpleasantness of work, and uncertainty represent nonvertical dimensions. Thus, it is no surprise that the hierarchical measure of prestige is found to be very positively correlated (0.851) with occupational complexity, and also strongly associated with clerical ability (0.587). Because clerical abilities are highly associated with women, this finding helps us interpret the positive correlation between prestige and percentage female that has been found elsewhere (Bose, 1973). Parcel and Mueller go on to suggest that the nonvertical aptitude/ability dimensions may underlie labor market segmentation theory and that the unpleasantness of work dimension is compatible with dual labor market theory.

Kolstad (1977) focused more on the income and education contribution to prestige. He found that as the proportion of women workers in a job increases, the more important are female earnings and the less important are male earnings in predicting prestige scores. Male earnings overestimate the earnings of workers, primarily women, in the pink-collar sector. Thus, while there is consensus that women's education and income contribute differently to occupational prestige than do men's, there is no consensus on the implications of this observation.

CONCLUSION

In sum, there has been controversy over whether or not prestige scores as conventionally used are equally valid for both genders. Many authors agree that they are valid if used only to study generalized social standing, while they should not be used in income-related social mobility studies. Others have observed that, particularly in gender-stereotyped jobs, prestige scores cannot be utilized in any circumstance because the ratings vary with both the gender of the rater and the gender of the job incumbent. Studies of the Duncan SEI and of similar indexes (Blishen, Nam and Powers) have already indicated the importance of using occupational data based on both men and women (either separately or for the total labor force) for their scores. It is now time to create a comparable contemporary version of prestige scores that reflect the occupational distribution and incumbency of women and men.

This study was designed to test assertions about the relationship of gender to occupational prestige, with data gathered at a point in time when the existence of married women's employment was widely accepted. The main objectives were to measure prestige for the full range of men's and women's occupations (including homemaker), to examine gender incumbency effects on prestige, and to develop a "Bose index" that would take into account any gender effects for all 1960, 1970, and 1980 detailed census occupations. Subsidiary goals included the examination of rater and job characteristics.

2

RESEARCH STRATEGY

This study is free of many of the shortcomings noted in the review of previous studies. It was based on a research design that combined the approach of controlled experiments with that of the sample survey. Carried out in late 1972, using a block quota sample of Baltimore, Maryland, adults and a sample of undergraduates from four schools in the same area, respondents were asked to rate the social standing of persons described on each of a set of 110 IBM cards. Each card contained an occupational title and information that indicated either a male or female incumbent or presented no incumbent information. This format gave no indication about the marital status of an incumbent so that family status would not contaminate the measurement of occupational status.

THE OCCUPATIONAL SAMPLE

The set of occupations used was selected to represent carefully the spread of occupations in the labor force and particularly the spread of gender-stereotyped occupations. Fifty occupations were chosen from the detailed 1960 census titles, with probability proportional to the percentage of males in the occupations. This was done by arranging all of the detailed occupations in order of the number of men holding each type of job. Five jobs were chosen from those census-detailed occupations, that represent the first 10 percent of all men who work. Another five jobs were chosen from among those categories that represent the next 10 percent of all employed men. This procedure was repeated for each decile of the distribution of men until 50 occupations were chosen. The process was then repeated to choose an additional 50 occupations with probability proportional to the percentage of employed women. Eight other occupations were added in order to include high-status jobs of special interest that are held by few and therefore rarely included in number-weighted samples. Finally, two roles indicating nonparticipation in the paid labor force were included. The first was "person living on welfare," and the second was household unpaid work, designated as "housewife/househusband," which varied depending upon the sex of the incumbent. This sample of occupations allowed comparisons among largely female, largely male, high-status, and unpaid occupations. Each respondent received a set of these 110 occupations.

The occupational sample represents the way in which men and women are spread throughout the occupational hierarchy. Each job chosen represented one of the detailed census categories. However, not all categories were represented, and some were included twice because they were selected from both the male and female job distributions. Some of these jobs are more illustrative of their source categories than are others. For example, "private secretary" clearly denotes the census category "secretary," whereas the category "ragpicker" less clearly exemplifies "managers, officials and proprietors, not elsewhere classified." This is not caused by sampling faults, but by the tremendous income and status variations incorporated within some of the census occupational codes. However, only four of the chosen occupations—ragpicker, stockbroker, administrative assistant, and powerhouse engineer—appear to be a poor fit to their source-detailed census category. Appendix B lists the jobs that were rated, their source in the detailed census occupational list, the percentage of women holding jobs in the detailed census category as of 1970, and the distribution (male or female) from which they were chosen.

The resulting sample of occupations, taken as a whole, turned out to be representative of the total labor force in both gender and prestige respects. The average percentage of women in the 108 labor force jobs, excluding housewife/husband and the welfare position, was 37.7 percent, exactly equal to the proportion of women in the paid labor force in 1970. The jobs ranged from those that had 0.7 percent female incumbents to those with as many as 98.5 percent women in the actual labor force. One-third of the jobs had less than 8 percent women, another third had between 8 and 51 percent women incumbents, and the last third of the jobs had greater than 51 percent women incumbents. Because the high-status jobs added to the sample had between 10 and 25 percent women in them, the middle range was somewhat compressed: Of the original 100 jobs, one-third fell between 8 and 61 percent women. Nonetheless, at least one-third of the jobs were dominated by women as incumbents, and almost two-thirds of the jobs were dominated by men. This sex segregation in our job sample accurately reflects the crowding of women into fewer occupations than those stereotypically available to men. In the total sample, 57 percent of the jobs were men's jobs in that they had 37.7 percent or fewer women incumbents (fewer than a random distribution of women over the age of 16 years in the 1970 labor force would lead one to expect), whereas 43 percent of the jobs in the sample were women's jobs. On the whole, the occupational set to be rated represented a wide distribution of labor force jobs according to their percentage male and female incumbents. Previous studies had selected fewer jobs and had tended to focus on the most highly sex-segregated ones.

Using previously derived NORC scores, it is also possible to estimate the status range of the occupations in our sample. The mean prestige score for all 108 labor force occupations is 39.8. The female-dominated jobs with more than 38 percent women have a mean prestige of 34.8 points, with a range from 13.6 to 63.1 points, whereas the male jobs have an average status of 43.6 points, with a range from 12.6 to 81.5 points. We see that the male jobs have an average of nine more prestige points than the female jobs. Examining the status range for male jobs, it is clear that their higher mean job status is based on male dominance of the more prestigious jobs. The highest-status women's job scores 63.1, whereas the highest-status men's job obtains a rating of 81.5. Thus, the most prestigious men's jobs score 18 points higher than jobs that women tend to enter.

THE MEASUREMENT OF GENDER

The gender measurement of the occupational titles was accomplished in two ways. First, from the relevant 1970 census tabulations, an "implicit" gender incumbency measure consisting of the proportion female actually holding each occupation was computed. Second, an explicit gender incumbency was given to some of the occupational titles by attaching a male or female name to them (for example, Barbara Wells, stock clerk; Kenneth Taft, box packer). There is considerable evidence that names are sensitive indicators of gender (for example, Fidell, 1970). Names used were chosen randomly, including primarily Anglo-Saxon-sounding names and excluding those appearing to have other ethnic connotations. Since ethnicities are known to vary in their relative status, we wanted to hold this variable constant. Names were used in order to prevent boredom on the part of respondents who would otherwise have had to read "female . . . (stenographer)," "female . . . (judge)," and so forth, 110 times. No one name consistently appeared with a given occupation in any of the respondent decks, the names being randomly assigned to an occupation. No one name appeared twice to the same respondent.

Gender measurement was also included in the sample design, utilizing both male and female respondents to rate the full range of sex-typed jobs with incumbents of varying genders.

THE EXPERIMENTAL TREATMENTS

Each respondent was assigned systematically to one of four treatments. Forty respondents were presented with 110 IBM cards containing occupational titles and female names. Another 40 respondents received cards that contained only male names and occupational titles. Eighty respondents received mixed card sets, one-half of which contained male and one-half female names and occupational titles. The remaining 40 respondents acted as a "control," with cards that contained occupational titles only. Within each treatment, one-half of the respondents were men and one-half women. The total design was equivalent to an experimental design with three treatments and a control group. Since men and women were equally and evenly distributed among the treatments, with the exception that the mixed-gender incumbent treatment received twice as many respondents, the design can also be treated as a ten-cell experiment, two additional cells being created by the cross classification of incumbent and respondent sex in the mixed-gender treatment. Although our plans called for 200 household sample respondents and 200 college sample respondents, actual fulfillment was slightly short of that goal: 197 householders (99 women and 98 men) and 195 students (111 women and 84 men). The household sample almost exactly approximated the ideal distribution of respondents, whereas the college sample reflected the ideal somewhat less accurately. The increase in the numbers of women in the college group could only improve the analysis, whereas the fewer numbers of men did no harm. College students sorted every card with an occupation on it, and householders sorted an average of 97.6 percent of the cards that they received. Thus, the total number of observations in the two samples were nearly identical, with 21,487 records for the household sample and 21,449 for the college group. The ideal, of course, would have been 110 occupations times 200 respondents, or 22,000 observations. Therefore, the total response rate was over 97 percent.

RESEARCH STRATEGY

THE RESPONDENT SAMPLE: HOUSEHOLDERS

Because occupational prestige scores have been shown in past stuies to be invariant over major population subgroups (Hodge et al., 1965) and anticipating this same invariance for female occupations and the effects of incumbent's sex on the ratings, we felt justified in using a small area sample from the city of Baltimore. The broad socioeconomic class base of this city was also an advantage. Block quota sampling was used with equal sex quotas. Blocks were chosen in proportion to the 1970 income distribution of the city census tracts to obtain an economic cross section. Only census tracts with 90 percent or more white population were used in order to reduce interviewing costs. [Since that time, other researchers have examined effects of the race of the rater and the race of a job incumbent on occupational prestige (see Sampson and Rossi, 1975).] Interviewers were instructed to seek respondents during both evenings and weekends as well as weekday daylight hours in order to obtain working persons in the sample. Only one adult (over 18 years) per household was interviewed and, if available, employed women were to be selected.

Twenty-eight percent of the resulting respondent sample were drawn from census tracts identified as lower income, 43 percent were from middle-income tracts, and the remaining 29 percent resided in upper-income tracts. The mean age of the sample was 41.5 years, with one-third of the group being younger than 29 and another third being 51 or older. Both the respondents' education and their estimated occupational prestige using NORC ratings (Siegel, 1971) of the 1960 census job titles varied according to their census tract of residence.

The respondents had completed a mean of 11.4 years of schooling, or slightly less than high school graduation. This is close to the 1970 national average of 11.7 years. On the whole, 58 percent of the sample had a high school diploma or more education. Turning to residential area, we found a mean of 9.4 years of education for respondents in the lowest-income tracts, 11.2 years for those in middle-income areas, and 13.7 years, or at least some college, among those from the upper-income tracts.

The pattern was similar for the respondents' estimated household status, which we designated with 1960 NORC scores. These scores were derived by Paul Siegel (1971) by averaging past prestige scores for jobs that could be allocated to each of the detailed 1960 census categories. Since those occupations are not necessarily representative of their category, we used the exact titles that were previously rated when they were available. If an occupation was not previously rated, Siegel's estimated 1960 ratings were used. Using this method the average household respondent's status was 42.5 on the NORC 100-point scale, with two-thirds of the group having a status of less than 46 points. Returning to the sampled income tracts, we found a mean score of 34.8 for respondents from the lowest-income tracts, a mean of 41.8 prestige points for those residing in middle-income tracts, and an average of 51.0 points for upper-income tract residents. These scores are significantly different from each other in the statistical sense, and are approximately equivalent to employment as a garage mechanic, a practical nurse, and a musician or stockbroker, respectively.

The distributions for respondents' status and education indicate that all economic and social classes were included in the household sample.

THE RESPONDENT SAMPLE: COLLEGE STUDENTS

The college sample was drawn from predominantly white colleges in and near Baltimore, including Towson State College, the University of Maryland in Baltimore County, and The Johns Hopkins University, to ensure some variety in the class background of student respondents. Seventy-two percent of the sample came from the state college, 16 percent from the state university, and 12 percent from the private university. Although the schools are predominantly white, 11 percent of the sample were black students, the majority of whom were women attending Towson State.

This sample had the advantage of holding both age and education variables relatively constant. Ninety-seven percent of the student sample was under age 30, and their average education was between 14 and 15 years. In contrast, only 35 percent of the household sample was under 30, and their average education was 11.4 years. The college sample was collected in anticipation that their ratings would differ from those of the general population. In an era of changing sex role definitions, changes would be more manifest among this young and highly educated sector.

There was nonetheless some social class variation among these students as one might find in a population sample. Using the 1960 NORC scores once again, we rated the occupational status of the students' households. Their mean status was 49.0 points. Parents of Towson State students scored 46.8, those of University of Maryland students scored somewhat higher at 51.2, and a more upper-class background was found among students at Johns Hopkins University (58.5). Only five of the respondents did not indicate a parental (or spouse's) job that could be coded to provide status scores; these respondents were assigned the mean score from their

RESEARCH STRATEGY

school. Similarly, missing cases in the household sample were given the mean score for their income tract.

Not surprisingly, the mean status of the college students (49.0) was higher than that of the household respondents (42.5). On the average, fewer working-class people were represented in four-year colleges than were middle- and upper-class persons. Even comparing householders under 30 years old with college students, we found a slightly lower status of 44.8 for the former group. Obviously many of these respondents had not had the opportunity to attend college and may have lacked access to higher-status jobs. On the other hand, respondents in the household sample who did hold a college or graduate degree had a high average status of 54.8. These people had a chance to turn their education into prestigious jobs, while college students had not yet had an opportunity to so do. Student status is still largely determined by parental occupations, which may be lower in prestige than the future ones of the students.

THE QUESTIONNAIRE AND RATING TASK

Both the household respondents and the college students were given the same actual task of rating the 110 occupations. Every respondent received a deck of 110 cards containing the occupational title and an indication of the sex of incumbent, where applicable. They also received a box with nine slots labeled from 1 to 9 in which they were to place the cards. The cards were prepunched so that they could be used in both self-administered and personal interview situations.

The task was presented to the respondents as follows:

People and their jobs differ in a lot of ways. We have made up descriptions of different kinds of people and their jobs. One of these descriptions appears on each card of the deck you have been given. You have also been given a box with slots in it; these are numbered from "1" to "9."

a. Please put a card in the slot labeled "1" if you think that the person with a job like that described on the card would have the highest possible social standing.

b. Please put a card in the slot labeled "9" if you think that the person with a job like that would have the lowest possible social standing.

c. If the description would belong somewhere in between, just put the card in the slot that matches the social standing of the person, somewhere between 1 and 9.

The respondents had no trouble doing this task. In response to closed questions, 96 percent of the college sample agreed that a prestige ladder of social standing existed and only 1 percent were not sure, whereas 92 percent of the household sample agreed and 6 percent were unsure.

A questionnaire, which was essentially the same for both samples, accompanied the card sort task. The household questionnaire was designed to be utilized in a personal interview situation and the college one for a self-administered format. Copies of the questionnaires appear in Appendix A.

Both questionnaires began with inquiries about the existence and justifiability of the existence of a "ladder of social standing." These items were intended to start respondents thinking about the nature of the problem given to them in the key card-sorting task. The question about the fairness of a prestige hierarchy was also useful in examining the variance among respondents in the range of scores they used. Those who believed the class system to be unfair may well have used a narrow range of ratings to indicate that all jobs have equal worth.

The next section of the questionnaire described the card-sorting task to the respondent. After completing this task, the respondents were asked a series of demographic questions including information on age, marital status, education (in the household sample), and current job. College students were asked about the employment of the head of the household in which they resided. A question on mother's employment and enjoyment of her work, where applicable, was also included because of prior evidence that attitudes toward women in the labor force are affected by parental attitudes toward working wives.

Both questionnaires concluded with three sets of items on general attitudes toward social standing, and particularly about gender and status.

The first set of questions (nos. 33-37 in the household questionnaire; nos. 12-16 in the college questionnaire) inquired into perceptions of the fairness of paying women less than men. Several different rationales were included as supportive of differential pay: women's supposed family responsibility, inability to do heavy physical labor, and lack of leadership roles. Assuming that respondents might accurately see women as being less valued by society in some occupations than men, this set of questions sought to discover the perceived fairness of such differential treatment. These questions were based on an exchange model of distributive justice in which justice exists if the rewards to a task are in a constant proportion to personal investment in that task. Although job investment by men and women is impossible to measure in any absolute sense, relative

RESEARCH STRATEGY

investment on the part of each gender is often imputed. Thus, the questions asked: If the income (or reward) going to a male and a female job incumbent is different, while the job is the same (or requiring the same investment), is justice occurring? If the answer was "yes," then the respondent was assuming the existence of differential investment or monetary needs on the part of women or men in the job. If the answer was "no," then the respondent was assuming the inputs of each person to be the same and there is something wrong with the conversion process from investments into rewards (such as income or prestige) when women are jobholders.

The next set of items (nos. 38A-F in the household questionnaire; nos. 17A-F in the college questionnaire) asked about the viability of occupational segregation or of having some jobs assigned as appropriate for members of only one gender. These questions served as a check on the card-sorting task by indicating if respondents felt there should be two separate labor markets, and perhaps separate status markets, divided according to sex-appropriate tasks.

The final set of items (nos. 39-45 in the household questionnaire; nos. 18-24 in the student questionnaire) inquired about the relative status of an individual employed in an occupation that is not typically held by a member of that gender. These questions served as a check on the rating task, but, more importantly, they inquired about the variable of incumbent's gender in atypical cases in which the most variation in prestige might be expected.

The total interview, including both the questionnaire and the sorting task, took from 30 to 60 minutes to administer in each sample. The sorting task took the bulk of the time, involving between 20 and 45 minutes.

MODE OF ANALYSIS

Multivariate analysis techniques, primarily regression, are employed with data resulting from the card-sorting task. The questionnaire data are used both in comparison to the results of the card-sort task and as added information on respondents' demographic characteristics or attitudes toward occupational prestige and equity.

The 1-9 ratings given to each card by the respondents were converted into the standard NORC prestige metric ranging from 0 (low) to 100 (high) (Siegel, 1971). The transformation used was the following:

$$\text{Prestige Score} = (9 - \text{Rating})12.5.$$

The resulting prestige scores for the original 110 occupations are presented in Appendix D. The appendix lists the scores separately by sample (household versus college) and by treatment (no incumbent, female incumbents only, male incumbents only, female incumbents rated in the mixed-gender treatment, and male incumbents as presented in the mixed treatment). It is these scores that are the subject of the analyses in Chapters 3-6.

In Chapter 3, on occupational prestige and gender, the unit of analysis is the individual prestige score, one for each of the 39,405 labor force occupation cards rated by the respondents. For each of the 108 occupational titles (excluding housewife/househusband and person living on welfare), the average no incumbent (control) prestige score from our study is also used in the analysis as a control variable. Without these scores, very little of the variance is explained, since occupational characteristics absorb most of the rating variance. The new no incumbent scores are better for this purpose than prior NORC scores because the control scores were developed for a representative sample of gender-stereotyped jobs. In fact, use of the standard NORC scores is confounded with the independent variable of percentage female. The general model used in this chapter is as follows:

$$P_{ij} = NOINC_i + \sum_{k}^{k} b_k T_k + \sum_{j}^{j} b_j R_j + \sum_{s}^{s} b_s O_{si} + e,$$

where

P_{ij} is the prestige score given to the ith occupational title by the jth respondent;

$NOINC_i$ is the no incumbent prestige score for the ith occupational title;

$\sum^{k} b_k T_k$ is the vector of k dummy variables, indicating the treatment under which the prestige score was obtained;

$\sum^{j} b_j R_j$ is a vector of j variables relating to respondent characteristics;

$\sum^{s} b_s O_{si}$ is a vector of s occupational characteristics for the ith occupation;

e is the stochastic error term.

Thus, this model essentially estimates the ways in which prestige scores given to occupational titles vary from the control scores as a function of experimental treatments, characteristics of the

RESEARCH STRATEGY

occupations involved, and characteristics of the respondents who make the ratings. The model is applied separately to the household and college groups, and the resulting coefficients are compared.

The analysis procedure used regards each of the ratings as independent observations. But since each respondent contributed 110 ratings, and ratings of a respondent may be correlated with each other, the observations are nonindependent to the extent of intrarater correlation, an effect similar to cluster sampling. In parallel studies (Rossi and Nock, 1982), "experiments" with subsamples of independent ratings (obtained by taking only one rating from each respondent), the effects of intrarater correlations were found to be negligible. Furthermore, the analysis procedure used here was found to overestimate standard errors and hence constituted a conservative bias. (The standard error of the estimate would be of the order of 0.01 prestige point.)

Chapter 4 builds on the previous analysis by focusing on the major non-labor force occupation of housewife/househusband. Here the prestige of nonpaying roles for men and for women is examined, and a prestige score suitable for status attainment studies is presented. Housewife and househusband are compared with their equivalent jobs in the labor force. This indicates their likely income if such roles were monetarily compensated and provides one way in which to independently estimate their prestige.

Next, the prestige standings of housewife and househusband are compared with those of other gender-stereotyped roles in the labor force. Although individuals do not necessarily choose jobs because of their social standing alone, it is possible to examine the status "trade-offs" for women and men of being in or out of the labor force. Of course, a comparison with the other non-labor force role, person on welfare, also gives the reader a sense of the status incentives accorded persons of varying social class and gender. For each of these descriptive analyses, occupational prestige is calculated by finding the mean prestige accorded a job by all respondents within a given treatment. In other words, the cell mean for these nonpaying roles is compared with those for paid employment.

However, for the final analysis of rater effects, the actual scores given by a respondent to the housewife or househusband are regressed on each individual's characteristics.

Chapter 5 explores the relationship between education, income, and prestige. The relationship between previous NORC scores, the Duncan SEI, and the Bose no incumbent prestige scores is first described. Then the no incumbent prestige scores, as well as those scores with an incumbent, are each regressed on median education and income for the appropriate gender. In order to perform comparisons with the original Duncan scores, 1960 data are initially utilized. The comparative beta weights and unstandardized coefficients for male and female income and education indicate the importance of each of the variables for men and women in the labor force and reveal the differences found when using incumbent prestige scores. The differences are also explored separately for gender-stereotyped jobs.

This chapter is particularly important for those who have relied on Duncan scores of socioeconomic status, since the method of derivation is the same but the gender of the incumbent is now taken into account. The chapter describes the derivation of an alternative scoring system, the Bose scores, already in use with data from the National Longitudinal Surveys (NLS). A comparison of Bose, Duncan, and Siegel/NORC scores is provided in Appendix C, whereas Bose scores for the three-digit detailed census occupations of 1960, 1970, and 1980 are constructed and then presented for male and female incumbents in Appendix E. The 1970 and 1980 scores have never previously been available, and the scores for all three census decades should be particularly useful for survey researchers wishing to code male and female occupational prestige. Equations are provided to project scores for those jobs that may not be included in the appendix.

An individual level analysis is presented in Chapter 6, focusing on respondent consensus with the average or normative ratings and on the variation in consensus about jobs. The dependent variable in the former analysis is the correlation between an individual respondent's occupational ranking and the average scores given by all others in the same experimental treatment. The independent variables include the respondent's own prestige, gender, age, education, and attitudinal variables.

After determining the degree of respondent consensus on the prestige hierarchy, the degree of consensus across occupations is examined by comparing the standard deviations around mean occupational prestige ratings. The differences accorded female and male incumbents will be a particular focus in order to test the stability of changes in attitudes toward women's employment in both traditionally female and nontraditional jobs.

Finally, Chapter 7 summarizes the important points of the monograph, discusses the issues raised, and indicates uses of this research as well as potential directions for future work.

3

PRESTIGE AND GENDER: THE INCUMBENT, THE USUAL INCUMBENT, AND THE RESPONDENT

The actual prestige scores derived by the methodology described in Chapter 2 appear in Appendix D, where they are presented for each occupation separately by experimental treatment and by respondent sample. The main question to be addressed in this chapter is whether those prestige scores given to labor force occupations are affected by the gender of an incumbent designated as occupying that position. The gender of the respondent and the implicit gender of the usual incumbent, measured by percentage female, are also of concern. The general model used in this analysis is the one outlined in Chapter 2, as follows:

$$P_{ij} = NOINC_i + \sum_k^k b_k T_k + \sum_j^j b_j R_j + \sum_s^s b_s O_{si} + e,$$

where

P_{ij} is the prestige score given to the ith occupational title by the jth respondent;

$NOINC_i$ is the no incumbent prestige score for the ith occupational title;

$\sum_k^k b_k T_k$ is a vector of k dummy variables, indicating the treatment under which the prestige score was obtained;

$\sum_j^j b_j R_j$ is a vector of j variables relating to respondent characteristics;

$\sum_s b_s O_{si}$ is a vector of s occupational characteristics for the ith occupation;

e   is the stochastic error term.

The specific content of this model can be divided into several groups of variables, including treatment, respondent, and occupational characteristics.

The treatment variables consist of a set of dummy variables indicating the gender of the respondent and the gender of the incumbent designated on the card being rated. The omitted category in this case is the control treatment in which no incumbent was specified. Initially the treatment variables were included as noninteracting dummy variables: sex of respondent and a female or male incumbent, with the no incumbent category omitted. These results showed no significant effect of respondent's gender in the college sample, but did show that the presence of either a female or a male incumbent would significantly lower scores (by -2.67 and -2.49, respectively) for all respondents. However, in the household sample, sex of respondent did have significant impact (women gave ratings -0.72 lower than men's) as did the presence of female incumbents (rated 1.66 higher than the gender-neutral scores). Male incumbents indicated no significant impact. Because of this, it appeared necessary to use respondent/incumbent interactions, particularly for the household sample.

Individual characteristics that are a priori related to prestige judgments are included as respondent variables. Since the respondents' ratings of the cards could be influenced by their own social standing (Hodge and Rossi, 1978), a score representing the prestige of the respondent's household is included.* Respondent's age is also included because attitudes toward women's labor force participation have been shown (Roper Organization, 1980) to vary by that characteristic as well. Members of the college sample, expected to be more egalitarian in their views toward gender treatment, are indicated by a dummy variable when the two samples are combined; and years of education is included for household sample members.

A personal ideological component was added to the individual variables using two attitude measures: (1) a "fairness" question, asking whether the respondent thinks that the existence of a hierarchy of social standing is fair or unfair; and (2) a "sex inequality" item,

---

*Computed according to the findings shown in Nock and Rossi (1978).

TABLE 3-1

Regression of Prestige Ratings on Occupation, Treatment, and Respondent Characteristics

Independent Variables	Total Sample		College Sample		Household Sample	
	b	SE	b	SE	b	SE
Occupational Characteristics						
NOINC score	0.939***	0.0045	0.945***	0.005	0.933***	0.007
Percent female	0.018***	0.0028	0.023***	0.003	0.013**	0.004
Treatment Characteristics [a]						
Respondent / Incumbent						
Male / Male	-1.932***	0.325	-2.935***	0.410	-1.134*	0.499
Male / Female	-0.151	0.325	-2.509***	0.410	1.869***	0.501
Female / Male	-1.129***	0.317	-2.151***	0.387	0.049	0.506
Female / Female	-0.786*	0.316	-2.790***	0.383	1.425**	0.504
Respondent Characteristics						
Household prestige [b]	0.042***	0.007	0.044***	0.008	0.034**	0.013
Age	-0.019*	0.009	-0.223***	0.030	0.001	0.010
Education (years)	-0.643***	0.045	—	—	-0.557***	0.057
College sample [a]	-9.459***	0.663	—	—	—	—

(continued)

TABLE 3-1 (continued)

Independent Variables	Total Sample		College Sample		Household Sample	
	b	SE	b	SE	b	SE
Black[a]	-0.541	0.451	-0.294	0.397	—	—
Sex equality	0.637**	0.202	1.100***	0.247	0.109	0.319
Fairness	0.216*	0.106	0.960***	0.128	-0.617***	0.170
Intercept	10.044***	—	5.832***	—	8.226***	—
R^2	0.534***	—	0.607***	—	0.478***	—
n	39,405	—	19,655	—	19,750	—

NOINC, no incumbent.
*$p < 0.05$
**$p < 0.01$
***$p < 0.001$
[a]Dummy variable. Coded 1 = College; 1 = Black; 1 = Female.
[b]A composite household score based on the occupational and educational attainments of household members (see Nock and Rossi, 1978).

which directly asks whether a woman holding the same job as a man should be accorded the same, lesser, or greater social standing. A positive value on this scale indicates willingness to accord equal or higher social standing to a woman. This item ascertains explicitly held values relating to the implicit nature of the rating task. The questions were asked only after the rating task was completed.

The main occupational characteristics included are the gender-neutral prestige score and the proportion female among actual incumbents in an occupation (implicit gender incumbency measure).

Using these occupational, respondent, and treatment variables, we can now describe gender effects on incumbent prestige scores for the 108 labor force jobs. Table 3-1 shows the regression equation resulting from our model.

INCUMBENT GENDER EFFECTS

The left-hand column of Table 3-1 represents the total sample. The -9.5 coefficient for the college sample, the largest for any dummy variable, hints at the usefulness of examining the two samples separately (in the second and third columns) to check for the hypothesized sample interaction effects. College students rate incumbents significantly lower than the household sample, even net of the variables in the model (see constants), supporting our contention that gender-focused prestige studies done with students are not easily generalized to other populations. However, these lower ratings are consistent with the significant negative coefficient for education in the household sample.

Among other similarities between the samples, occupational characteristics have significant impact on the ratings. As expected, the no incumbent (NOINC) scores dominate the equation, indicating that most respondent judgments of an occupation are influenced by the general societal consensus about where the occupation in question stands. All told, 48 and 61 percent of the variance in the ratings given to the cards by the household and college groups, respectively, is explained by the equation, with about 1 and 2.5 percent, respectively, of the variance in the samples being accounted for by the independent variables, exclusive of the gender-neutral scores. Apparently prestige is founded largely on class-based aspects of occupations rather than on incumbent or rater characteristics. Note that the "implicit gender incumbency" measure, proportion of female incumbents, also has significant regression coefficients, with more salience (a larger b) for the college group. While female-dominated jobs gain prestige, the maximum possible gain is about one to two points for 100 percent, as compared with 0 percent female jobs.

This advantage is numerically comparable to the effects of a female job incumbent, which can represent a gain from 0.4 to 3 points over a male incumbent.

Interestingly, if Siegel's NORC scores are used in this equation instead of the new no incumbent scores, the percentage female shows no significant impact (treatment effects remain similar). This is a result of holding NORC scores constant. These traditional scores give a composite rating to each occupation derived from ratings of comparable jobs dominated by men that are classified in the same census category as any particular (male- or female-dominated) title. Thus, the effect of percentage female is largely factored out if NORC scores are used, since women are underrepresented, supporting the argument that a male bias is built into existing scores. Further, the treatment effects garner about 10 percent of the variance because the NORC scores leave out gender effects.

Returning to Table 3-1, note that the effects of the treatment characteristics for incumbent and respondent gender and their interactions are small and contain some surprises. First of all, male respondents tend to give slightly lower ratings than female respondents, but uniformly lower ratings to occupations with explicit male incumbents. In contrast, female respondents tend to give higher ratings to titles with explicit female incumbents. Second, there are differences between the two samples surfacing around the dummy treatment variables, which are consistent and strongly negative for the college sample, indicating that college students are likely to downgrade all of the cards on which any incumbent is designated. Perhaps the presence of any person in a generalized role, or a note of reality, downgrades the role. Male students downgrade female incumbents less than male incumbents, but female students downgrade female incumbents more than they do male incumbents. In contrast, the Baltimore household survey results show that both male and female respondents give higher points to female incumbents, a tendency to favor women that is stronger among male than among female respondents. Further, only men rating male incumbents give scores below the neutral ones, whereas both women and men rate female incumbents significantly higher than the control scores. The household sample clearly feels that a female incumbent in a job adds to its status, at a rate approximately equal to the effect of anyone holding an all female job.

It should be noted that none of the coefficients involved is very large. Thus, all men tend to rate male incumbent occupations about one to three prestige points lower than titles that have no incumbents, and women in the household sample rate male incumbent occupations about the same as occupations with no incumbent designation. The two-point spread is statistically significant but not very much, considering that the total scale ranges from a high near 90 to a low near 8. These findings indicate that little variation in the prestige of occupations can be accounted for by the implicit gender composition of the occupation or by the addition of a gender-marked incumbent.

Only slightly more of the variance in ratings is accounted for by respondent characteristics. The higher the household social standing of the respondent, the more likely they will rate an occupation higher. Although the increment is not very great—for each household prestige point, respondents rate each title 0.034-0.044 higher—the range in household prestige also has to be taken into account. Thus, between those at the very bottom of the scale, households living on welfare, and those in top-rated households with two professionals, there is an average difference of about three prestige points in their respective ratings of all occupations.

Respondent age affects college student but not the Baltimore household ratings. However, educational attainment is influential for both. In short, the better educated accord less prestige than do the less educated, and the impact of education is larger than that of gender.

Blacks in the college sample do not significantly differ from white students in their ratings.

Finally, moving to the attitude scales, another difference between the two samples surfaces. Among the college students, persons who believe in equal or better treatment for women in jobs tend to give significantly higher scores to all occupations, but this tendency is not replicated among the Baltimore household survey respondents. Among college students, those who believe the existence of a prestige scale is fair give an additional point to scores, whereas household respondents feeling the same way deduct 0.6 point from their ratings. Although it is understandable that a belief in equality and fairness would add points to the students' scores, it is less clear why a belief in the fairness of a hierarchy would deduct points from the householders' scores. However, this downgrading and attitude/behavior problem represents a smaller numerical effect than that of other variables.

In sum, occupation explains most of the variance in incumbent prestige scores. Percentage female and an actual female incumbent can add up to three points each to incumbent ratings. This is significant statistically, but small compared with the impact of the gender-neutral scores. In fact, the education of the rater can have a larger impact than gender.

Sex of incumbent affects both women and men as raters in each sample; however, the impact is largest in the household sample, and especially among male respondents. Household respondents uniformly and to a greater extent favor female incumbents, whereas college students tend to favor only slightly those of the opposite gender. College students thus exhibit somewhat greater equality in their evaluations of male and female incumbents than do householders who give any woman holding a job "extra" status above the gender-neutral titles. On the other hand, both household and college sample members are affected by the percentage female on the job.

It should also be noted that the amount of variance explained by the two equations differs by almost 13 percent, with more of the variance being explained in the college sample as compared with the household sample (61 as compared with 48 percent). The error variance for the college sample is correspondingly lower. Since other studies have shown that the better educated have lower error variance in studies of this sort (see Hodge and Rossi, 1978), this finding is not unusual.

SEX SEGREGATION: STATUS OF WOMEN'S AND MEN'S JOBS

In past NORC prestige ranking tasks, women's jobs were not systematically included. By doing so in this study, it is possible to accurately assess the relative prestige distributions for women's jobs as they compare with men's jobs. For these purposes, women's jobs are defined as those with 37.7 percent or more female incumbents and male jobs are those with 37.7 percent or fewer women, where 37.7 percent was the percentage of women in the total 1970 work force.

There is actually no consensus on how to define operationally women's and men's jobs. Jusenius (1975) followed a method similar to the one used in this volume, defining those jobs with 48.1 percent or more women (38.1 percent average plus an additional 10 percent) as female occupations, those with 28.1 percent or less women (38.1 percent average less 10 percent) as male occupations, and those between 28.2 and 48 percent as mixed occupations. Oppenheimer (1970), alternatively, defined female jobs as those with 70 percent or more female. Functionally there is little difference, because so few jobs are actually mixed. Using Oppenheimer's definition, the 29 women's jobs in our sample would have a mean prestige of 39; using Jusenius's definition, the 39 women's jobs would have a mean prestige of 36; and using our definition, the 46 women's jobs have an average prestige of 38. The range of prestige scores for men's and women's jobs is identical under all three definitions. Thus, we proceed using a definition of stereotyped jobs as those with a greater percentage of men or women than expected, based on average representation in the labor force.

The no incumbent treatment from the household sample is the appropriate comparison base with previous studies. In this treatment, the 46 women's jobs have an average prestige of 38 and a range of 8-75. The 62 men's occupations have a mean prestige of 50 with a range of 5-96. Traditional jobs are detrimental to women's status attainment in two ways. First, the average prestige in female jobs is 12 points lower than in male jobs;* and second, the maximum achievable prestige within the traditional women's labor market realm is a fully 21 points below that attainable within traditional male jobs (75 vs 96). These differences are statistically significant. It appears that those who have been advocating the importance of women entering nontraditional fields have been correct.† Similarly, those who have suggested that the expanding women's sector has lower esteem are validated.

To provide concrete examples of the types of jobs implied in this analysis, Table 3-2 presents the ten jobs in the set studied herein that have the highest concentration of women and the ten jobs with the highest concentration of men. Between these most stereotyped jobs, an average prestige difference of about seven points is found. Given these differences, we are not surprised that the variable of percentage women usually holding an occupation (implied incumbent) is statistically significant in Table 3-1. However, in Table 3-1, the impact of percentage female is positive, adding up to

---

*Average prestige is computed as a straight average across gender-typed jobs and is not weighted by the proportion of women or men in each of the occupational titles. Weighted figures yield average prestige scores of 42 for women's and 46 for men's jobs. Because women numerically cluster in midlevel service and clerical jobs, the weighted average gives a false impression of high average status for women and ignores the small variation in the status of female-stereotyped jobs.

†However, even this may not prove a useful strategy by which to gain status. In response to questionnaire item no. 43, 33 percent of the household sample thought that women in traditional men's jobs would have lower standing than male incumbents in such jobs. On the other hand, the questionnaire item highlighted the anomaly of such a situation. The majority of the respondents expected equal male and female status in these gender-stereotyped jobs, and the actual ratings given are quite egalitarian.

TABLE 3-2
Prestige Scores (from Control Treatment[a]) for Jobs with High and Low Percentages of Women Jobholders

Jobs with High Percentage Women	Percentage Women (1970)	Prestige Score	Jobs with High Percentage Men	Percentage Women (1970)	Prestige Score
Housekeeper	98.5	25.3	Floor finisher	1.6	28.8
Dental assistant	97.8	54.8	Garbage collector	1.6	16.3
Private secretary	97.6	60.9	Electrical engineer	1.6	79.5
Office secretary	97.6	51.3	Building construction contractor	1.5	78.9
Babysitter	97.5	18.3	Truck driver	1.4	40.1
Registered nurse	97.3	75.0	Powerhouse engineer	1.4	64.5
Floor supervisor in a hospital	97.3	60.3	Auto mechanic	1.3	44.9
Practical nurse	96.4	56.4	Carpenter	1.3	53.5
Maid/Household dayworker	96.0	11.5	Plumber	1.0	58.7
Dress cutter	95.1	33.3	Locomotive engineer	0.7	52.9
Average prestige		44.7			51.8

[a]Treatment in which no incumbents were shown on cards. Household sample.

two points to the prestige of a job. We see this effect within women's jobs, where all women's jobs have an average status of 38 but the ten most concentrated women's jobs have an average status of 45.

This effect does not hold up as well between men's and women's jobs. In fact, percentage female is negatively correlated with job status. The zero-order correlation (r) between percentage women and no incumbent prestige is -0.20 over the 108 labor force occupations, but the effect holds mainly for high-status jobs. Within jobs in the bottom or middle thirds of the prestige ranking, the correlation between percentage female and standing is near zero ($r = -0.02$ and 0.03, respectively). Only in the top one-third of the jobs are prestige and percentage women significantly and negatively correlated at $r = -0.29$. This is almost inevitable since the highest-ranked "women's job" has a prestige score of 75, and top-ranked men's jobs have low percentages of women. Thus, percentage female increases job prestige only for traditional women's jobs, and the advantage is lost outside this boundary. We therefore agree with England (1979) that women are underrepresented in prestigeful jobs, but disagree on the impact of percentage of women in a job on its prestige.

Given this variation in occupational effect by level of prestige, the next section explores whether the effects on ratings of the sex of the incumbent or of the respondent's sex might also vary with job rank or each other. However, note that within both male and female gender-stereotyped jobs, female incumbents are given two additional points by household respondents (as for all jobs), whereas college respondents are more egalitarian and do not distinguish ratings by gender of incumbent at all. Thus, the effects of implied sex of the incumbent (percentage female) are independent of actual job incumbent.

GENDER AND THE JUDGER

There is sufficient reason to suspect from the results of Table 3-1 that men and women may well be judging the occupations differently. There is also evidence that respondents' socioeconomic levels affect ratings as well. Accordingly, Tables 3-3 and 3-4 separate respondents by gender and by household prestige, respectively. In both tables, each column contains the results of regressing the prestige scores on the variables shown.

In Table 3-3, the implicit (percentage of women) and explicit (incumbent) gender of a job each interacts with respondent gender. Within both household and college samples, women, and not men, upgrade jobs more than the average rater according to the extent to

TABLE 3-3

Regressions of Prestige Ratings on Respondent and Other Experimental Characteristics by Respondent Gender for Each Sample

	Household Sample		College Sample	
	Female Resp. b, (SE)	Male Resp. b, (SE)	Female Resp. b, (SE)	Male Resp. b, (SE)
Experimental Characteristics				
NOINC rating	0.960*** (0.009)	0.848*** (0.010)	0.932*** (0.007)	0.888*** (0.008)
Percentage female	0.017** (0.006)	-0.015* (0.006)	0.021*** (0.005)	-0.005 (0.005)
Male incumbents	1.474* (0.605)	-3.100*** (0.634)	-0.995* (0.486)	-4.401*** (0.522)
Female incumbents	3.034*** (0.610)	0.164 (0.642)	-1.446** (0.480)	-3.62*** (0.519)
Respondent Characteristics				
Household prestige	0.055** (0.017)	0.062** (0.021)	0.033** (0.011)	0.071*** (0.011)
Age	0.004 (0.159)	0.013 (0.014)	-0.261*** (0.041)	-0.250*** (0.047)
Education	-0.959*** (0.089)	-0.369*** (0.080)	— —	— —
Black	— —	— —	-2.807*** (0.473)	6.929*** (0.785)
Sex equality	0.867* (0.434)	-0.827 (0.475)	1.121** (0.328)	1.148** (0.403)
Fairness	-0.723** (0.233)	-1.045*** (0.258)	0.665*** (0.180)	0.996*** (0.189)
Intercept	8.691***	11.947***	7.343**	9.891***
R^2	0.511	0.437	0.597	0.601
n	10,381	9,783	11,550	8,470

Resp., respondent; NOINC, no incumbent.
 *$p < 0.05$
 **$p < 0.01$
 ***$p < 0.001$

which the job is female dominated. The statistically significant effect of percentage female noted in Table 3-1 is caused largely by women valuing more highly the usefulness or worth of their own traditional occupations. Household men significantly downgrade women's jobs, whereas college men ignore this characteristic.

On the other hand, both women and men are influenced by gender of incumbents. In the household sample, women give male incumbents 1.5 points and female incumbents 3.0 points more than the control scores; men are unaffected by a female incumbent, but deduct 3.1 points from male incumbent scores. Thus, household women are especially sensitive to female incumbents and give them three extra points, whereas men are sensitive to male incumbents and deduct three points. Neither college men nor women greatly differentiate between male and female incumbents.

No single explanation accounts satisfactorily for the divergent rating tendencies of men and women. The best proposal is that women respondents are replicating findings of other studies showing that raters tend to upgrade their own occupations, assuming that women are responding empathetically to all female incumbents. But contrary to expectations, male respondents appear to be downgrading occupations with male incumbents.

Few other characteristics interact with sex of respondent in either sample. Race of respondent has opposite effects for college students. Black women downgrade occupations, whereas black males upgrade them. Black women appear to follow the pattern of those with higher education in general, but the responses of the few black men are harder to interpret, given the small case base. Sex equality also has differential gender impacts. Household men's belief in equality or more status for women does not affect their ratings, whereas it makes all other respondents, logically, attribute higher prestige in general.

Since family status or household prestige may also interact with types of ratings given, each sample was next partitioned at the mean respondent household prestige, with the results indicated in Table 3-4. As with the highly educated, more variance is explained for those coming from higher prestige backgrounds.

In the college sample, high-prestige students give additional points to female-dominated jobs, but do not differentiate at all between male and female incumbents, whereas low-prestige respondents differentiate slightly in favor of actual male incumbents and ignore implicit incumbency.

High-prestige householders are similar to high-prestige students in the significant positive impact of implicit gender, but they are similar to male householders (who probably hold most high-status jobs) in significantly lowering male incumbent scores. Low-

TABLE 3-4

Regressions of Prestige Ratings on Respondent and Other Experimental Characteristics by Household Prestige for Each Sample[a]

	Household Sample		College Sample	
	High Prestige b, (SE)	Low Prestige b, (SE)	High Prestige b, (SE)	Low Prestige b, (SE)
Experimental Characteristics				
NOINC rating	0.938***	0.885***	0.906***	0.922***
	(0.010)	(0.009)	(0.007)	(0.009)
Percentage female	0.017**	-0.008	0.016***	0.001
	(0.006)	(0.006)	(0.004)	(0.006)
Male incumbents	-2.963***	0.907	-2.034***	-3.061***
	(0.612)	(0.594)	(0.450)	(0.559)
Female incumbents	1.148	2.410***	-1.941***	-3.730***
	(0.615)	(0.595)	(0.446)	(0.558)
Respondent Characteristics				
Household prestige	0.258***	0.053	0.036**	0.137***
	(0.022)	(0.028)	(0.012)	(0.031)
Age	0.007	0.024	-0.360***	0.463***
	(0.015)	(0.015)	(0.033)	(0.075)
Education	-0.839***	-0.290**	—	—
	(0.080)	(0.084)	—	—
Black	—	—	1.058	-0.260
	—	—	(0.630)	(0.577)
Sex equality	1.497**	-1.202**	-0.524	4.027***
	(0.482)	(0.419)	(0.314)	(0.420)
Fairness	-1.051***	-0.641**	0.345*	1.807***
	(0.244)	(0.231)	(0.160)	(0.222)
Sex of respondent	-3.767***	0.927*	-0.732*	0.834
	(0.504)	(0.427)	(0.328)	(0.447)
Intercept	0.779	6.915***	10.926***	-8.215**
R^2	0.566	0.434	0.601	0.599
n	7,021	13,093	12,209	8,811

[a] Household prestige dichotomized at median score of 45.3.
*$p < 0.05$
**$p < 0.01$
***$p < 0.001$

prestige householders, like women, give more points to female incumbents. This pattern is repeated in the effect of sex of respondent, where women from low-prestige families give more points than men, and women in high-prestige households give fewer points.

Turning to other respondent characteristics of these prestige groups, one finds similar effects, particularly in the impact of education. Here, the negative effect of age in the college group holds up only for high-status students, and there are some attitudinal effects whereby high-prestige householders and low-prestige students who feel that women deserve higher status than men in jobs do accord that extra status.

On the whole, the interactions by gender of respondent are somewhat larger than those by prestige background of respondent. In all cases, the differences are more pronounced for implicit and actual gender of incumbent than for other characteristics, and they are greater in the household than the college sample. The level of impact is the same as noted in Table 3-1, although incumbent gender can add as much as two or three points to control scores and female-dominated jobs can gain up to two points.

CONCLUSION

The original question on the relationship of gender to occupational prestige is not answered simply. Examining men and women in the same jobs, nonincumbent occupational prestige is revealed as the major determinant. All of the gender factors combined contribute between 1 and 2.5 percent to the variance in incumbent prestige scores. However, all the gender factors are significant.

These findings support the theoretical assumption that incumbent prestige ratings represent achieved occupational status as modified by ascribed sex of incumbent, rather than as some more equal mix of gender prestige and occupational prestige combining to form a new social standing variable. Occupation remains the major contributor to prestige, or the repute an individual can gain through positions held. This is similar to other job evaluation situations, such as those being developed to measure comparable worth, where the current incumbent is of little import, but the aggregate effects of usual incumbent are visible in salary, task ratings, etc.

Many pieces of information are taken into account by respondents when they subjectively rate occupational prestige, among which are race and gender of the actual incumbent, gender of the usual incumbent, income reward of the job, education required, and importance of the job to society. To a certain extent, "pure" occupational prestige has never been measured. However, the methodology used here allows the separation of effects of actual and usual sex of incumbent on job prestige.

In general, the gender impacts are positive in predictable ways or neutral. First, gender of incumbent affects householders' ratings, with female incumbents given an average of two more points than males. Male respondents do this by lowering male incumbent scores, and female respondents do so by raising female incumbent scores. Women's response is interpretable as upgrading their own occupations, whereas the cause of male "chivalry" is less clear from these data. Since chivalry often reflects the presumed higher status of the giver, men may be indirectly recognizing their own status. In contrast, college students do not utilize most data on gender and make their prestige judgments largely unaffected by sex of incumbent or their own gender. Their response may predict a change in trend for the future, or reflect the effects of higher education, liberal thought, and, to a certain extent, inexperience with job discrimination. Second, we find that sex composition and segregation influence both female and high-status raters in each sample to give about two additional points to women's jobs. This effect appears to hold up within women's jobs, but not between men's and women's jobs: The mean and range of prestige for predominantly female jobs are lower than those for men's jobs. So, whereas women accord more status to their own traditional jobs, the reality of lower incomes also places a ceiling on additional prestige given. On the whole, gender components may add or subtract only about two points from an occupational prestige score, indicating that occupational prestige standing is not as sensitive to gender as it is to respondent education and the basic distribution of jobs. It is for this reason that Chapter 6 further discusses respondent variation and consensus.

The near equity in subjective occupational repute is unrelated to the actual resources of jobs. Women's incomes remain lower than men's, and, as illustrated in Chapter 5, their income and education combined explain less variance in prestige scores than do the income and education of men. Gender impacts are thus larger for objective than for subjective status scores, especially when income is one of the prime determinants.

Finally, there are two methodological conclusions, related to sampling, which can be drawn from this analysis. First, results from the many prestige and gender studies carried out on student populations may not generalize well to other groups, as was previously assumed. College students and highly educated household sample members give lower than average ratings to any incumbent. This unrepresentativeness is further corroborated by the more egalitarian ratings of college students, which ignore sex of incumbent. Second, it is imperative that gender and prestige studies use samples of jobs reflecting the labor force distribution and including a full range of sex-stereotyped jobs. Previous studies, using only very stereotyped jobs, found more exacerbated differences in prestige than when all jobs are included. Further, existing NORC scores, based on samples of male-dominated jobs, mask the impact of percentage female since they already indirectly control for this effect. The new no incumbent scores, based on a better sample, do not do so and thus are more appropriate.

4

SAME ROLE, DIFFERENT PRESTIGE: THE HOUSEWIFE AND THE HOUSEHUSBAND

Over the last decade, stratification studies of women's economic role have finally included the previously ignored occupation of housewife. Yet there is still much disagreement on both the components of the homemaker role and the function this job has in the larger stratification system. Resolution of these questions is important for social mobility studies as well as for occupational studies of this most widely held U.S. job. Most studies have assumed that the only way in which women obtained status was through a paid labor force job or via their husbands. "Time out" from the labor force was viewed as a gap in individual status-gaining roles, which caused methodological and measurement problems for mobility studies. While a solution to a male military service gap was found, no one tried to develop a means of solving the female home service gap. By developing a single social status score for the homemaker role and comparing this prestige to other occupational alternatives, the analysis in this chapter facilitates a solution to such problems.

The titles of "housewife," "househusband," and even "person living on welfare" are chosen because they lack the ambiguity of a "not working" status and because each implies the possibility that the individual could participate in the labor force. For example, a

---

*Portions of the analysis in this chapter represent an edited version of Christine Bose, "Social Status of the Homemaker," pp. 69-87 in <u>Women and Household Labor</u>, edited by Sarah Fenstermaker Berk. Copyright © 1980 by Sage Publications, Inc. Reprinted with permission of Sage Publications, Inc.

person who is retired or totally disabled would not be in the labor force and would be unlikely to obtain a job. However, an adult on welfare may have the capacity to hold a job, if one were available with sufficient income. Similarly, a homemaker may or may not be employed, depending upon the availability of child care, the accessibility of jobs, and the desire or the economic need to work. Of course, other non-labor force roles, such as living on dividend income (formerly called being a "capitalist"), also imply the ability to work. However, this particular role has previously been rated and is not key to our concern with the relationship of gender to prestige.

THE STATUS OF HOMEMAKING

In the no incumbent treatment of this study, where respondents are comparing housewife or househusband with other jobs, the average occupational prestige score is 45. However, household respondents rate housewife at 51 on the scale and househusband at 15. The difference is not quite as dramatic in the college group, where housewife is accorded 46 and househusband 32 points. The general low ranking of the househusband is not a surprise, since the role lacks cultural legitimacy. In fact, such men are so rare that there is no real term for male homemakers. We defined it for our respondents as "someone who keeps house while (his) wife works."

On the other hand, a rating of 51 or 46 for housewife at first seems fairly high, given that an employed housekeeper rates only 25-29 points. Even though the housewife's score was near that of an average job, previous research would lead one to expect a lower evaluation of housewives—an evaluation that would approximate that of a housekeeper. Yet in the past there were few job opportunities for women, particularly married women, in the labor force, and women's work at home was arduous (Strasser, 1982). The higher status of a housewife could be viewed as a substitute reward for this labor. Although women receive no cash wages for their home labor, they do receive large amounts of status for staying out of the "rat race" and not competing with men. Ehrenreich and English (1975) stressed that women themselves, at the turn of the century, tried to improve the status of the housewife and to professionalize the role. The domestic science movement of the period sought to develop an appreciation of the volume of scientific knowledge (such as the germ theory of disease) that was necessary to be a competent homemaker. To a certain extent, men accepted this movement, for it channeled the drive for women's access to higher education into the traditional field of home economics, and thus back into the home itself. The rating may also be due to weighting differentially some higher-status components of housework, such as childrearing, over other lower-status components, such as scrubbing floors. Thus, the housewife role may be given extra moral status because of its frequent association with motherhood.

However, there is no consensus on the housewife's prestige. When measured across all treatments and respondents, housewife had a variance of 1,018, while most occupational variance was in the 300-500 range. The second largest variance (876) was for the artist role, and another dozen occupations fell into the 600 range, including coal miner and then farmer, househusband, landscape gardener, social worker, and sociologist. This latter group fell at all levels of the prestige scale, so that the lack of consensus on the status of such jobs cannot be attributed to merely falling in the middle of the prestige scale where more variation is possible. The dispersion is more related to confusion over the content of these occupations, making it difficult to place them on a prestige scale. A further discussion of consensus and labor force jobs is continued in Chapter 6.

In the case of the housewife, each of the nine slots in the rating box was used by some respondents. The modal response was slot 5, but slots 1, 5, 6, 7, and 9 all received ten or more votes and included 71 percent of the household sample respondents. In the absence of further information about the housewife's own education or her spouse's occupation, respondents may be saying "phooey" (slot 9), "average" (slots 5, 6, 7), or "great" (slot 1). The 51- and 46-point ratings do not appear to be the result of respondents averaging all possible husband's jobs and attributing the "average spouse" to the wife. Instead, there appears to be substantive disagreement about how to rate housewife and, implicitly, about which elements of that work role are salient for prestige ratings. Some of this difference in perspective can be accounted for by rater characteristics, as will be shown below. For the moment, this chapter will focus on the average no incumbent prestige and compare it with that of other occupations.

STATUS EQUIVALENTS OF THE HOMEMAKER ROLE

Housework is work that deserves to be rewarded for its own sake, and not just for keeping women out of the paid labor force. The position minimally involves being a housekeeper, maid, laundress, cook, waitress, practical nurse, elementary school teacher, seamstress, chauffer, administrative assistant, and so on. These tasks are repeated seven days a week, often for more than eight hours per day, and can include over 70 discrete tasks per day.

SAME ROLE, DIFFERENT PRESTIGE

One way to determine housewife's prestige might be to compare it with its labor force equivalent. "Housekeeper" alone does not define all of the comparable labor force roles. Housekeeping activities such as cleaning and laundering are involved in housework, but cooking, shopping, caring for children, nursing, and administrative skills are also included. Other aspects, such as straightening up or nurturing, have no labor market equivalent. Thus, the housewife role is greater than the sum of its market-defined parts. One can find only a rough labor market equivalent of the role. One way to do this is to select the labor force occupations in the study that best approximate a housewife's role and find the average no incumbent status of these jobs. Fifteen jobs were chosen for this procedure, and Table 4-1 indicates the resulting approximation of a housewife's status if housework were considered a labor force role. The household average is 35 points, or 16 points fewer than the housewife actually receives, whereas the college average is 39 points, or 7 points less than actually given. Are these 16 and 7 points an incentive to women to stay out of the labor force? Are they a bonus to women for bearing children, which even male househusbands cannot achieve? Or is the housewife obtaining more status than one would expect?

These may be the wrong questions to ask. More important is that the housewife is grossly underrewarded for the significance of the work she does. Recent insurance estimates indicate that a full-time housewife and mother works 100 hours per week. At a minimum wage of approximately $3.50 per hour, the housewife deserves $18,200.00 per year. Even taking the lower estimates made of the housewife's average work week as 55 hours (Vanek, 1974), a $10,010.00 annual income would be earned.

Another way to approach the question of economic value is to explore the income and educational components of social standing. Blau and Duncan (1967) found that prestige scores, such as the household no incumbent ones described here, were related to male education and income by the equation:

$$\text{Prestige} = 0.59X_2 + 0.55X_3 - 6.0,$$

where

X_2 is the percentage of men in a job with greater than $3,000 earnings per year;
X_3 is the percentage of men with a high school diploma or more education.

To use this equation for female homemakers, substitute for X_3 the 52.3 percent of all working women who have at least four years

TABLE 4-1

Average Status of No Incumbent Jobs Roughly Approximating Duties of a Homemaker

Occupation	Household Prestige	College Prestige
Boardinghouse keeper	24	35
Housekeeper	25	29
Maid	12	22
Laundry worker	15	18
Textile machine operator (e.g., seamstress)	28	37
Short-order cook	22	24
Pastry chef	39	43
Waitress	22	28
Hairdresser	39	43
Delivery truck driver (an approximation of chauffeur)	27	29
Babysitter	18	20
Grade school teacher	65	65
Social worker	63	63
Practical nurse	56	60
Administrative assistant	68	63
Average of above occupations	35	39

of high school education and replace X_2 with the $0 earnings of housewives. The result is the low status of 23 prestige points. This is the prestige one might expect a housewife to receive based upon her income. To examine the expected income based on prestige, substitute for X_3, assuming a status of 51 points for housewife, and then solve for X_2. Now one finds that 48 percent of all housewives should be earning more than $3,000 per year, according to the household sample. These projected earnings are close to, but below, the current claims of pay due housewives. Note that these calculations are based on conversion factors for men of income and education into prestige. This basis assumes that women earn prestige from their incomes and education in the same way that men do. This assumption is probably false, especially because of the low variance in women's income. It does, however, give housewives all the advantages of men in the paid labor force. If the prestige scores of all 108 labor force occupations as measured in the mixed incumbent treatment for female incumbents are used to develop a new equation usable for women, we find this relationship:

Prestige = 5.54(Median Education of Women in Job)
+ 0.0048(Median Income of Women in Job) − 34.4.

Substituting for the mixed incumbent housewife prestige of 44 in the household sample, the housewife achieves a median income of $2,292 in 1960 dollars. Given current inflation, the 1970 figure would probably fall betweeen $3,000 and $4,000, and the 1980 figures would more than triple that.

On the whole, female homemakers do receive more status than those holding equivalent labor force roles and less pay than those with equivalent status. They also receive considerably more status than do others who remain at home: Househusbands obtain 15 prestige points from householders and 32 points from students, whereas persons living on welfare obtain only 8 points from householders and 4 points from students.

STATUS ALTERNATIVES TO THE HOMEMAKER ROLE

The disagreements among researchers on the status of the housewife may stem not from a variation in the perceived status of housewife, but from the variation in other status options available to women. Table 4-2 presents a listing of women's occupations rated by householders as having higher no incumbent prestige than the housewife. The college group would include three additional jobs: typist, keypunch operator, and bookkeeper. In this case, as in the previous chapter, women's occupations are defined as those in the job sample with greater than the percentage of women that are in the labor force.

The 51 prestige points of a housewife may be close to the average rating of all jobs, but it is quite high as compared with the prestige of jobs that most women enter. As shown in Table 4-2, the highest-ranking traditional women's job is registered nurse, with 75 points. In fact, only 30 percent of women's jobs rank higher than housewife. To obtain status higher than a housewife, women can go into any of the traditional female fields of secretary, nurse,

TABLE 4-2

Women's Occupations with No Incumbent Prestige
Higher Than Housewife or 51 Points
(Household Sample)

Occupation	Prestige
Office secretary	51
Inspector in a manufacturing plant	51
Stenographer	53
Dental assistant	55
Practical nurse	56
Floor supervisor in a hospital	60
Private secretary	61
Hospital lab technician	63
Social worker	63
Hotel manager	64
Grade school teacher	65
Administrative assistant	68
High school teacher	70
Registered nurse	75

teacher, lab technician, and social worker. Or they can try to fight remaining opposition in a male job. All these jobs require training and the money available to spend on education. Not all families can afford to supply this training. So the housewife status could be an attractive alternative to women who cannot afford the educational investment or who find the only jobs available to them are deskilled and unchallenging. This explains why working-class women accept housewife status, as described by Komarovsky (1962). Blue-collar wives may feel trapped or bored with housework tasks, but they do value the role of housewife. This makes sense for two reasons. First, the cleaning, shopping, and other household tasks they perform are not very different from the manual tasks their spouses do at work. Second, without further education, they could not obtain a job with higher prestige than that of housewife. Thus, the housewife's prestige, near that of an average job, is attractive to working-class women.

Middle-class college-educated women or women who have held professional jobs at one time, such as those described by Lopata (1971) and by Oakley (1974), feel housewife status to be a low one, even at an average of 51 points. Their perspective on the same homemaker role is different because they have the education that gives them access to higher-status positions in the labor force. If they want to have the most status possible, they should be in the labor force and not in the home. So it should be no surprise that middle-class women report dissatisfaction with the housewife role. This tendency is not reflected, however, in a depression of the actual prestige score attributed to housewife. In fact, those respondents ranking housewife in the mid-to-upper levels were those from higher-prestige families. (Householders with prestige of less than 42 rated housewife at an average of 41 points, whereas householders with prestige above 42 rated housewife at 59 points.) Therefore, it is clear that middle-class women are looking down on housewifery only as it compares with their other role options. In fact, even at 59 points, housewife looks better than many more labor force options than it did at 51 points.

Relatively few women in traditional women's jobs have higher status than a housewife. Why do so many women choose jobs having lower status than housewife? There are several answers. First, and most obvious, is that status is not the major motivation in making decisions. Women often work to provide needed income for a family. At least 60 percent of women who work are single, widowed, or divorced or have spouses whose income is inadequate to support a family. Second, education level predicts when women will enter the labor force, with those having higher education being more likely to use it. Third, although there are intrinsic rewards as well as status bonuses for a housewife, worth in U.S. society is defined primarily by economic gain. There are no direct economic gains paid to a housewife unless she enters the labor force. An outside job also allows women to meet more people and to have a greater variety of tasks to perform. Once children are in school, there is less to occupy one's time in the home. Then the labor force becomes an even more attractive alternative, regardless of the job. Thus, working-class and single women are likely to work for money, and middle-class women may seek to use their educational training as well. Both groups are more likely to seek employment if previously employed themselves or if their mothers held paying jobs. Both groups work for job satisfaction and to reduce social isolation.

Interestingly, men do not have the slight status alternatives that women have. Househusband, the equivalent of housewife for men, receives 15 points in the household sample and 32 points in the college sample. From the point of view of the household group, the only male jobs with less prestige are ragpicker (5 points), parking lot attendant (8 points), bellhop (11 points), and janitor (12 points). The predominant ideology stresses that all men should work in the labor force unless physically incapable of doing so. The homemaker position is allotted to millions of women capable of paid employment. Yet, if a man is a homemaker, it is assumed that he could and should be holding a paid position and that he is shirking his duties. He therefore is not given much status for being a househusband. In fact, the househusband's status is very similar to that of a person on welfare (eight points). In order to obtain either income or status, men must be in the labor force.

Once again, we find the college sample to be more egalitarian than the household group. While they rate person on welfare at the very bottom, with only 4 points, they do accord the househusband 32 points. This is not as much as they give to the housewife, but it is significantly more than householders give to a househusband. In fact, there are 15 traditional men's jobs with status lower than househusband, including garbage collector, coal miner, cotton farmer, delivery truck driver, rubber mixer, and others. Clearly, these students see a househusband as having more status than many traditional male working-class jobs.

EFFECTS OF RESPONDENT CHARACTERISTICS

Since the status of the homemaker varies so greatly with the gender of the incumbent (housewife versus househusband), the obvious next step is to ascertain if the gender of the respondent also affects the ratings.

Househusband's prestige shows almost no fluctuation: Male and female householders rate it at 15 and 14, respectively, whereas male and female college students allocate 33 and 30 points each, respectively.

On the other hand, gender of respondent affects the prestige of the housewife more than it impacts any other role. The 51 average score given by householders is caused by the high rating given to the role by women (61) and the rather low rating given by men (41). The pattern is similar among college students, where the 46 average prestige results from a 52-point rating by the women and a 40-point rating by the men. Although a definite interpretation of these results is not allowed by the data, it can be hypothesized that women, particularly in the household group, are able to bring non-labor force considerations to their ratings of the housewife role. For example, they may focus on the positive cultural aspects of motherhood. In the no incumbent treatment, women are not clearly presented in other jobs, and the positive rewards of the home are not brought into direct comparison to the economic rewards of the job market. In fact, college women, who may have immediate employment plans and thus are already making such comparisons, rate housewifery lower than do women from the household sample (52 vs 61).

Other experimental treatments help to test this thesis. In the treatment where every job is presented with a female incumbent, women household respondents drop their rating of the housewife by 10 points to a rating of 51. In the mixed-gender incumbent treatment, household women's ratings drop another 14 points to 37. This is in concurrence with male and female students, who both rate the role at 36 under these circumstances. At the same time, household men raise their estimation of housewife to 50 points. Apparently, in the abstract situation, women rate housewives highly, but when forced to compare homemaking to a mixed-gender labor force in which they would have a myriad of job options, women drop their rating of the role to 36 or 37. This low rating given by all women and by college men does reflect accurately the lower status of housewifely tasks when performed for pay. These scores are roughly the same as the status of 35 or 39 obtained by averaging the labor force components of homemaking (see Table 4-1).

The contextual effect is therefore extremely important in determining the prestige accorded to housewives. It is primarily the change in women's perceptions that causes the drop in housewife's standing between the no incumbent and mixed incumbent treatments. In fact, male household respondents prevent the aggregate score of housewife from dropping much below the mean of all occupations in the mixed incumbent situation. These men appear to prefer to accord a woman more status as a housewife than as a competitor in the labor market. All other groups concur that housewife has a lower equivalent labor market prestige. The mixed incumbent finding is similar to earlier research such as that by Menger (1932), who discovered that although housewife ranked in the middle of her occupational sample, there was great disagreement even then as to the status of the role, with men rating it high and women rating it low.

For the purposes of mobility studies, the household mixed-gender treatment probably presents the most accurate picture by which to compare the housewife role with paid labor force roles. In this case, the average prestige score assigned by men and women is 44, with men slightly overrating the job and women underrating it. In this treatment, the status of househusband is fairly stable: 24 in the household sample and 27 in the college group. It still appears

TABLE 4-3

Regression of Housewife Rating on Respondent Characteristics (Household Sample)

Variable	Unstandardized Coefficient	Beta
Age	0.52	0.28*
Household status[a]	0.51	0.25*
Marital status[b]	-11.51	-0.17
Mixed incumbent[c]	-7.35	-0.11
Years of education	1.05	0.13
Housewife[d]	5.92	0.09
Intercept	2.69	—

$R^2 = 0.20$; n = 97.
*Significant at 0.05 or better.

[a] Prestige of head of household.
[b] Coded 1 = married; 0 = single, separated/divorced, widowed.
[c] Dummy variable for effect of mixed incumbent treatment where 1 = mixed treatment, 0 = all other treatments.
[d] Response to question, Are you working? Coded 1 = fulltime housewife, 0 = all others.

to maintain an element of social opprobrium, but begins to approximate the composite labor force homemaker score of 35.

Although respondent's gender clearly influences the rating given by householders to housewives, multivariate analyses result in the disappearance of its effects when controlling for other related variables. Regressing housewife prestige ratings given by all householders on their demographic and attitudinal attributes, shown in Table 4-3, results only in age and status of household contributing significantly at the 0.05 level. Older respondents and those households headed by high-prestige occupation holders appear to rate housewives higher. Although not statistically significant, housewives and those with high education also value the role. As noted above, the mixed incumbent context does lower housewife prestige. But surprisingly, married persons rate housewife fully 11 points lower than nonmarrieds.

The exact effects of household head's status are difficult to decipher. As indicated earlier, ratings of housewife tend to clump around the two ends and the upper middle of the prestige scale. Those persons ranking housewife low tend to be of low status themselves, and those rating housewife higher tend to have high occupational standing. However, a distribution of average household status according to attributed housewife rank shows the relationship is not directly linear. Those from households with head's status below the mean for the sample (42) show the most confusion or dispersion in their judgment. They rate housewife at 41 with a variance of 1,193. Those from households above the mean status give housewives 59 points with a variance of 635. Thus, middle-class people rate housewife rather highly, and working-class people tend to rate housewife 18 points lower, but some rate her highly as well. Nilson (1978) suggested that the role may be a luxury in a time when most families need two incomes, and thus it would be rated highly. Fulltime housewifery will be more of a luxury for working-class people who seem to be torn between rating a working-class housewife as low as her comparable labor force options and rating her high because she represents such a luxury. Thus, Nilson's analysis seems to explain lower-class respondents' variance in housewife status.

Because some of the variables in Table 4-3, such as being a housewife, vary with respondent's gender, separate regression analyses were performed for male and female householders. Only age significantly affects men's ranking of the housewife. The prestige of their jobs, marital status, and education all have no effect. For women, holding a current or prior job is the most important predictor of the housewife's score. If a woman has been employed, the housewife score dramatically drops 41 points. Years of education, household head's status, age, and marital status prove insignificant for women, though married women still tend to rate housewifery low. Further analyses show that while the absolute prestige level of a woman's labor force job does not affect her ratings of the housewife role, it is more important than level of spousal prestige.

Thus, although both age and occupational considerations are important in the overall rating process, there are sex differences in their relevance. For women, respondent characteristics explain more variance (35 percent) than do comparable variables for men (18 percent).

In summary, women who have held labor force jobs are greatly affected by the employment experience, no matter what the prestige of the job, and thus rate the housewife role lower than those who have remained at home. In this way, employed wives are similar to college women. Nonetheless, the higher the status of the job held (or the higher the class background a woman has), the more positively she will see housewifery. Nonmarried women and housewives themselves also rate the role more highly.

CONCLUSION

It is now possible to assign a single numerical prestige score to the roles of housewife and househusband. To the extent that the household sample is representative of the general population, a score of 51 out of 100 prestige points can be assigned to the housewife; and for purposes of comparison with labor force roles, such as for social mobility studies, the score of 44 (as derived from the mixed-gender rating situation) seems appropriate. Similarly, househusband may be assigned a score of 15 or 24. If one feels that the college group represents the trend of the future, then their attribution of 36 points to the housewife and 27 to the househusband (from the mixed-gender treatment) may be the most appropriate for mobility studies.

Exactly how a woman views the homemaker role depends on her job options and need for income. The status of housewife is higher than most working-class women's jobs, but lower than most middle-class women's jobs. So the former are likely to be satisfied with the role and the latter dissatisfied. Further, those who have been in the paid labor force are likely to be so dissatisfied as to lower their ratings of the housewife. Although status maximization is not a major motivation for everyone, it does influence decisions and perceptions of one's options. Exactly how men view the role depends primarily on their age.

A housewife's status is higher than recent writers would lead one to expect and certainly is higher than labor force jobs such as housekeeper. This positive trade-off can act as an incentive for women not to compete for scarce labor force occupations or as a reward for a household not needing a second wage earner. On the other hand, the low status of a househusband can force him to enter the labor force to gain either prestige or income. Women do achieve more status than one would predict, perhaps because of childrearing, but they also receive no income for their roles. Thus, they gain status in compensation for their loss of income. Whether or not the status gain is actually given for motherhood is a task for future research. This hypothesis could be tested by analyzing the variance in prestige received by housewives with various numbers of children.

Certainly, we already know that child care is the household area around which people feel the most affect.

The status of a housewife is high, but few women achieve higher status when entering the labor force, especially since the prestige range of the frequently entered women's occupations is limited. Thus, the social status of homemaker is a stick to men and a carrot to women. It can cut competition for a limited number of jobs and can help obtain much work in the home, needed by society, without having to pay for it.

Certainly homemaking is work, but the contextual effects of the work help determine exactly what status it is accorded. For example, when it is compared with a labor force job, its status drops. The status of the homemaker could change. If many of a housewife's tasks, such as laundry, food preparation, and child care, were taken over by others in the paid labor force, leaving primarily consumption and nurturing work in the home, it seems likely that the status of housework would drop. Although consumption and family support are important to the U.S. economy, they are not regarded as complex and productive work. If a household's tasks were actually shared among its members, the housewife/househusband role might disappear. However, lack of any real change in recent household division of labor makes this unlikely. As real wages decline in the United States, an increasing number of women are entering paid work while continuing to do housework. Therefore, it seems reasonable to expect that there will indeed be an increasing class convergence in how housework is viewed.

5

THE RELATIONSHIP OF INCOME, EDUCATION, AND PRESTIGE: THE BOSE INDEX AND DUNCAN SCORES

In this chapter, attention is turned to the general problem of extrapolating prestige scores for men and women holding jobs that are not included among the 108 labor force occupations utilized in this study. Methods of predicting such scores are useful in social mobility research. The social standing scores most commonly used are the NORC prestige scores (Siegel, 1971) and the Duncan socioeconomic scores (Blau and Duncan, 1967). The prestige scores constructed in this study are compared first with past NORC prestige scores and then with the Duncan SEI scores. Finally, new scores are projected for the 1960, 1970, and 1980 census occupations.

THE RELATIONSHIP BETWEEN NATIONAL OPINION RESEARCH CENTER AND NO INCUMBENT SCORES

The no incumbent (or NOINC) treatment in this study most closely approximates the previous NORC scores because they were also derived from occupations rated without an incumbent. The no incumbent treatment is thus the intermediary link between past NORC scores and those computed from this study for incumbents.

The table in Appendix C compares the Baltimore householders' no incumbent ratings with the estimated NORC scores for each occupation in our survey. The NORC scores were computed for the detailed occupational 1960 census categories by Paul Siegel (1971) using an estimation procedure. He averaged the prestige scores of any job that had ever been rated within each census category to arrive at a score for the entire category. For our sample, which was also derived from the 1960 detailed categories, NORC scores were first

INCOME, EDUCATION, AND PRESTIGE

assigned to jobs that had been explicitly rated in the past. Where no perfect fit was available, Siegel's prestige estimates for the detailed census category were used. The occupations in Appendix C are arranged in ascending rank order as rated in the household no incumbent treatment. The household, rather than the college, sample is used as the basis of comparison because it more closely approximates the population from which the NORC scores were obtained.

The NORC scores for the 108 occupations have a mean prestige of 40 as compared with an average of 45 points for the householders' ratings and 46 among the college students. The NORC scores are correlated at $r = 0.90$ with householder ratings and at $r = 0.91$ with college student scores, whereas the householder and student occupational prestige ratings correlated with each other at a nearly perfect $r = 0.98$. Thus, the ordering of the jobs is most similar between the two samples that use the incumbent method, but the relationship of NORC to no incumbent scores is strong as well. There are a few jobs for which NORC scores do not accurately represent no incumbent prestige. For example, four occupations (ragpicker, stockbroker, administrative assistant, and powerhouse engineer) have NORC scores that are 20 points or more different from their householders' no incumbent ratings. When these four occupations are dropped from the sample, the correlation between NORC and no incumbent scores increases from 0.90 to 0.94.

Other differences between the ratings derived in this study and the NORC scores are caused partially by an underrepresentation of female jobs scored using NORC methods and by Siegel's estimation procedures, which resulted in a large amount of variance in the prestige of jobs in any given census category.

The status distribution of jobs in each study also affects the correlation. In this study, the highest-prestige jobs are professor, mayor, and physician. In past NORC occupational studies, these jobs have been near the top, but other roles, including Supreme Court justice, governor, and cabinet member, were also included. These latter roles achieved the highest NORC scores. Since the prestige metric reaches its maximum at 100, the occupations of professor and physician are consequently placed lower in the NORC metric than they are in the current no incumbent scores, reducing the correlation between household sample scores and previous NORC scores. On the bottom end of the metric, our study includes two occupations, ragpicker and person on welfare, which have lower status than any other previously measured job. They act to stretch the scale in the opposite direction and to further reduce the correlation.

On the whole, more jobs received no incumbent ratings above, rather than below, their NORC estimates, producing a higher mean prestige for the former. The household scores become increasingly higher than their NORC estimates above the level of 21 prestige points.

THE RELATIONSHIP BETWEEN DUNCAN AND NO INCUMBENT SCORES

Duncan's SEI for occupations was initially developed to predict prestige scores for any given occupation that a man might hold. Since its development, other researchers have used the index to study female mobility patterns. Among the first were deJong et al. (1971). How appropriate is this? To answer this question, one must examine the development of the scores.

Duncan developed the index by regressing NORC prestige scores (which had no incumbent) on the education and income of men actually holding each job. The equation resulting from this sample of jobs was used to project SEI scores for all occupations. The independent variable measures were the percentage of men in each job with greater than $3,000 earnings per year and the percentage of men with a high school diploma or more education, each standardized by age. The job was the unit of analysis, and none of the variables were weighted in proportion to the numbers of persons in each job.

These measures present several problems for the study of female mobility. First, Duncan's use of the early sample of NORC jobs meant that women's jobs were underrepresented. Second, Duncan did not compute SEI scores using income and education measures for female incumbents in particular or for the total labor force. For his study of father-to-son mobility, he did not need this information. In fact, the NORC jobs he used to develop SEI scores were presented in a context implying a male incumbent, making the usage of male education and income data appropriate. Yet Duncan's SEI scores were used by others to study women's occupational mobility; and it is only recently that women's wage and income data have been considered in the development of new socioeconomic scores (Stevens and Featherman, 1981; Nam and Powers, 1983).

One advantage of the incumbent prestige scores constructed here is that they facilitate a comparison of Duncan's male-based status scale with another similar one based on female data. SEI scores can be projected from the representative 108 jobs, as rated by the household sample, using separate income and education data and no incumbent (or incumbent) prestige for women and men. We do this below with 1960 data in order to remain parallel to Duncan's original analysis. Data for 1970 and 1980 are incorporated later.

INCOME, EDUCATION, AND PRESTIGE

Our measures differ slightly from Duncan's by focusing on the median values for women's and men's income and years of education. The median is appropriate because it is more easily interpretable than "percentage of persons above 'X' level of income," which also introduces homoscedasticity into the regression equations. Further, varying the income or education cutoff levels to fit with the current economy changes the values of the raw regression coefficients and would make comparisons over time more difficult.

Median earnings for those in each census detailed job category are measured for persons over age 14 in the 1959 experienced civilian labor force who worked 50-52 weeks. Using fulltime workers makes the earnings of women and men more comparable than would the inclusion of the many parttime women workers. Median education is measured for all persons over 14 years in the 1960 civilian labor force, since education is less likely to vary by work status.* Neither education nor income is standardized by age in this analysis because Duncan found that age contributed only about 3 percent of the variance in the scores. As for Duncan, the job is the unit of analysis here and no weighting procedure is used.

Turning to the actual data, the average 1960 median male income for the 108 sample occupations is $5,237 and the average median female income is $3,402, whereas the median male education in the jobs is 11.53 years and female education is 11.55 years. These sample means are not statistically different from the population means. The standard deviation of women's income ($1,272) is smaller than that of men ($2,058), implying that the lower income is found no matter what the status of the job. On the other hand, there is little dramatic difference between employed men and women in their education level.

Income and education are highly correlated with prestige, ranging from $r = 0.65$ to $r = 0.81$ as shown in Table 5-1. For both men and women, education is more strongly related than is income to prestige. This is not surprising, since prestige taps job aspects beyond their purely economic rewards. The prestige and income correlations are significantly higher for male jobholders than for females. This may imply that women's income is more randomly related to prestige than is men's income; but since there is less variance to begin with in women's earnings, it is most probable that female income is less capable of varying in a patterned way with prestige. Although there are female/male differences in the corre-

---

*Data are from the U.S. Bureau of the Census (1963, see Tables 9 and 30).

TABLE 5-1

Correlations Among Median Income, Median Years of Education, and Prestige of Job by Gender of Incumbent (Household Sample)

Prestige	Median Education in Job		Median Income in Job	
	Female	Male	Female	Male
No incumbent	0.77	0.80	0.66	0.70
Mixed incumbent (female)	0.78	—	0.65	—
Mixed incumbent (male)	—	0.81	—	0.71

n = 108 occupations.

lations, within gender groups the no and mixed incumbent correlations are similar.

Keeping all of this background information in mind, Duncan's process can now be replicated using data on men and women, with a more representative job sample and for both mixed and no incumbent prestige.

First, no incumbent prestige is regressed on median years of women's education and on median women's income of those actually holding each job, as reported in the 1960 census. The following relationship is found:

NOINC Prestige = 0.0055(Median Dollars Income of Women)
+ 5.60(Median Years Education of Women) - 38.5.   (1)

Next the process is repeated for men in those same jobs, and the resulting relationship is the following:

NOINC Prestige = 0.0039(Median Dollars Income of Men)
+ 4.97(Median Years Education of Men) - 32.8.   (2)

When Eq. 2 is used to project scores for the 108 labor force occupations, the new ratings approximate the original Duncan SEI scores. For purposes of comparison with NORC and no incumbent prestige scores, these SEI scores are provided in Appendix C.

Since prestige scores vary slightly, based on the gender of the incumbent, the above analysis is performed again using the male and female incumbent prestige scores derived from the mixed-gender

INCOME, EDUCATION, AND PRESTIGE

treatment that best approximates a mixed-sex labor force. Regressing mixed incumbent female prestige on median women's education and income of those actually holding each job, the resulting relationship is:

Mixed Female Prestige = 0.0048(Median Dollars Income of Women)

+ 5.54(Median Years Education of Women) − 34.4.   (3)

Using mixed incumbent male prestige and male data, the equation becomes:

Mixed Male Prestige = 0.0038(Median Dollars Income of Men)

+ 4.70(Median Years Education of Men) − 28.2.   (4)

Note that in both pairs of equations, the intercept for women is lower: Women tend to start at a lower level of prestige than do men and thus have a harder time catching up. Income is not actually much help to women in determining prestige since the variance in their economic rewards is much lower than for men. Although the raw income regression coefficients are larger for women than for men, the standardized coefficients are lower for women (0.31 and 0.29) than for men (0.36 and 0.36) in both the no and mixed incumbent treatments, respectively. Education is a slightly more important determinant of prestige than income, but it helps women and men fairly equally, with betas of 0.55 each in the no incumbent situation and of 0.57 for women and 0.54 for men in the mixed incumbent equations. On the whole, income is more important for men than for women in the prediction of prestige, whereas education is more equally important to both genders. Probably because of the difference in importance of income, more variance is explained for men (69 and 70 percent) than for women (64 and 63 percent) by the respective equations.

These differences are sufficient to suggest the use of separate equations for men and women jobholders when doing social mobility studies that determine prestige based on education and income data available for respondents. These findings also substantiate McLaughlin's work (1978) on the different task/income relationships existing within men's and women's jobs at the same prestige level. On the other hand, it casts doubt on any status scores for women's jobs such as Duncan's, which are generated based on the relationship of men's income and education to prestige in predominantly male jobs, such as the original NORC samples. Such a process overestimates women's status.

THE BOSE INDEX

Given these problems with SEI scores based on male data, the NLS have created a separate "Bose index" for the detailed three-digit occupational 1960 census categories using median female income and educational data. Regression Eq. 3 for women's mixed incumbent prestige is used to project new scores that are the equivalent of Duncan scores for women. The NLS use the index in association with occupations held by respondents in their young and older women's cohorts.* This "Bose index" is reproduced in Appendix E of this volume for the 1960 census occupations and can be used by mobility researchers.

The NLS Bose scores for women in occupations are correlated at $r = 0.79$ with the female mixed incumbent prestige scores. When equivalent Bose scores are derived for men, using male income and education data and male mixed incumbent scores as in Eq. 4, their correlation with the original prestige values is even higher ($r = 0.83$). The relationship between Bose scores and the original prestige scores can also be described in the following regression equations:

Female Mixed Incumbent Prestige = 1.0(Female Bose Index) + 0.04

Male Mixed Incumbent Prestige = 1.0(Male Bose Index) + 0.02.

The low intercepts indicate that the two sets of scores begin at roughly the same point; the slope of the regression lines (1.0) shows that the Bose and prestige scores increase at the same rate. The Bose scores appear to be an excellent approximation of the actual mixed incumbent prestige scores. Bose scores explain 63 percent of the variance for female incumbent prestige and 70 percent of the variance for male prestige. The correspondence between the two sets might be higher if women incumbents consistently received higher ratings than men. However, as indicated in Chapter 3, women incumbents lose some of their status advantage in higher-prestige, male-dominated jobs. This may introduce minor curvilinearity into the mixed incumbent scores, which is not preserved by linear regression. With this exception noted, the Bose scores can be said to reasonably approximate prestige scores for men and women.

---

*Details are found in the codebook for the NLS data set, available through the Center for Human Resource Research, Ohio State University, Worthington, Ohio.

INCOME, EDUCATION, AND PRESTIGE

Since prestige scores have, in the past, proven stable over time, while education and income regression coefficients vary, prestige scores appear to be a more stable reference for performing comparative research. Bose scores can therefore be created for each census decade (1960, 1970, and 1980) using the changing relationship among education, income, and incumbent prestige. Appendix E provides such Bose scores for the three-digit detailed occupational census categories of 1970 and 1980, as well as the NLS scores for 1960. The first step in the construction of the index is to develop equations that describe the relationship between incumbent prestige and occupational income and education data for women and men holding the 108 sample labor force jobs described here. Next those equations are used to project Bose scores for men and women in all census jobs. The process is similar to a construction of separate Duncan scores for men and women, using incumbent prestige as a dependent variable and with a full range of gender-stereotyped and -nonstereotyped jobs.

For 1970, data are available on the median earnings, school years completed, and weeks worked of all men and women in the experienced civilian labor force.* This allows the calculation of Bose scores for all employed men and all employed women. Since more women than men work parttime, the median income figures are not directly comparable. However, scores derived from these data accurately measure the average economic standing of women in an occupation.

To create an estimate of full-year earnings for both women and men, median income is also multiplied by the factor 50.0/median weeks worked. Because year-round employment is frequently compensated at a higher rate than part-year work, income will still be slightly underestimated. On the other hand, the median number of weeks worked for all employed women and men is 50. Therefore, the margin of error should be small. A second set of Bose scores is created using this full-year income data.

The two equations describing the relationship of incumbent prestige to 1970 income and education data for all employed workers are the following:

$$\text{Male Incumbent Prestige [or Male Bose Score]} = 5.40(\text{Median Male Years Education}) + 0.0026(\text{Median Male Earnings}) - 39.6 \quad (5)$$

---

*The data source is U.S. Bureau of the Census (1973, see Table 1, pp. 1-11).

Female Incumbent Prestige [or Female Bose Score] = 5.97(Median Female Years Education)

+ 0.0046(Median Female Earnings) − 47.3   (6)

The equations describing the relationship for full-year workers are the following:

Male Prestige [or Bose Score] = 5.37(Median Male Years Education) + 0.0026(Median

Male Earnings)(50.0/Median Weeks Worked) − 39.5   (7)

Female Prestige [or Bose Score] = 5.95(Median Female Years Education) + 0.0044(Me-

dian Female Earnings)(50.0/Median Weeks Worked) − 46.5 (8)

These equations are used to project the 1970 Bose indexes appearing in Appendix E.

As in the 1960 data, we see that women start from a lower prestige level and thus have a hard time catching up. Even with raw coefficients for education and income which are larger for women than for men, women's average Bose score is 39.5 compared with 49.4 for men. Among full-year workers, women close some of the gap, achieving an average score of 44.3 compared with men's 49.8 points.

The average Bose indexes for the 1980 census are more favorable to women, perhaps because there are fewer missing data on women in nontraditional jobs. The 1980 census reports separate occupational income figures for the total experienced civilian labor force and for year-round fulltime workers, facilitating the development of Bose scores.* However, the mean earnings rather than the median income are recorded, and median education had to be calculated from grouped data.

The resulting equations to describe the relationship of incumbent prestige, mean income, and median education for all workers in the 108 sampled jobs are the following:

---

*The income and education data source is U.S. Bureau of the Census (1984, Table 1, pp. 1-252). To develop equations 9 through 12, the original 108 occupations are matched to 1980 census categories using U.S. Bureau of the Census (1982).

INCOME, EDUCATION, AND PRESTIGE

$$\text{Male Incumbent Prestige [or Male Bose Score]} = 4.84(\text{Median Years Male Education})$$
$$+ 0.0013(\text{Mean Male Income}) - 38.1 \qquad (9)$$

$$\text{Female Incumbent Prestige [or Female Bose Score]} = 5.07(\text{Median Years Female Education})$$
$$+ 0.0028(\text{Mean Female Income}) - 44.0 \qquad (10)$$

The comparable equations for fulltime year-round employees are the following:

$$\text{Male Prestige [or Bose Score]} = 4.58(\text{Median Years Male Education})$$
$$+ 0.0013(\text{Mean Male Fulltime Income}) - 38.6 \qquad (11)$$

$$\text{Female Prestige [or Bose Score]} = 4.49(\text{Median Years Female Education})$$
$$+ 0.0027(\text{Mean Female Fulltime Income}) - 42.4. \qquad (12)$$

Both sets of equations are used to project Bose scores for all 1980 census occupations as they appear in Appendix E.

As before, women start from a lower prestige base than do men and appear to have higher income coefficients to help compensate for this deficit. However, in 1980 there are only small differences between men's and women's educational contributions to prestige. On the whole, women in 1980 obtain slightly higher average Bose scores than do men: 50.3 vs 49.3 among all workers and 50.7 vs 48.4 among fulltime year-round workers.

The three sets of Bose scores for 1960, 1970, and 1980 available in Appendix E should facilitate status attainment studies of women and men. As long as education and income continue to contribute differently to male and female employees' prestige, separate predictive equations or Bose scores are warranted. When only education and income data on respondents are available to the researcher, the predictive equations (Eqs. 3-12) can be used instead.

PRESTIGE, INCOME, AND EDUCATION IN GENDER-SEGREGATED JOBS

Separate equations for predicting women's and men's prestige, or projecting Bose scores, are not used because there are different "status markets," but because of the disparities in the labor market itself. A parallel situation to that of male and female incumbents exists among female- and male-dominated jobs, probably because of the higher income generally found in male-dominated or primary sector jobs. Women who are incumbents in traditionally female jobs have the following relationship among their income, education, and mixed incumbent prestige:

$$\text{Mixed Female Prestige} = 0.0027(\text{Median Dollar Income for Women}) + 5.9(\text{Median Years Education of Women}) - 33.1 \quad (13)$$

However, women in traditional men's jobs have a different relationship to the same variables:

$$\text{Mixed Female Prestige} = 0.0054(\text{Median Dollar Income for Women}) + 5.6(\text{Median Years Education of Women}) - 36.9 \quad (14)$$

Women in male jobs begin at a lower level of prestige than do those in female-typed jobs. In both job types, education is a better predictor of prestige (betas = 0.69 and 0.55, respectively) than is income (betas = 0.16 and 0.29, respectively). Education has a greater impact among female-dominated than among male-dominated jobs, whereas income has its greatest impact among male-dominated jobs rather than among women's traditional ones. Women's (and men's) income has less variance in female jobs, where there are also fewer career ladder opportunities than in male ones, and thus income accounts for less variance. Yet, on the whole, both income and education explain more variance for women in female (67 percent) than in male (59 percent) jobs. This suggests that there is discrimination against women in nontraditional jobs and that the increased random variation in women's prestige within male jobs, which is not attributable to income or education, is probably due to the gender of the incumbent.

MALE-BASED EQUATIONS AND FEMALE INCUMBENT SCORES

By now it should be clear that the relationship of prestige, income, and education differs for men and for women. Thus, it is inadvisable to use the equation predicting male incumbent prestige to develop Bose scores for women. If one substitutes female data in Eq. 4, which is derived from the relationship of mixed incumbent male prestige, income, and education, as follows:

INCOME, EDUCATION, AND PRESTIGE

$$\text{Male Incumbent Prestige \atop [or Female Bose Score]} = 0.0038(\text{Median Dollar Income of Women})$$

$$+ 4.70(\text{Median Years Education of Women}) - 28.2, \quad (15)$$

the resulting scores for women in the 108 occupations are depressed (mean 39) well below both the Bose index scores based on the appropriate equation (mean 46) and the actual female mixed incumbent prestige scores themselves (mean 46). Using the relationship among prestige, income, and education found for men to derive scores for women clearly underestimates women's actual prestige.

This underestimation can be illustrated in a second way. The male and female incumbent prestige scores are related to each other using this equation:

$$\text{Female Incumbent Prestige} = 0.97(\text{Male Incumbent Prestige}) + 1.4 \quad (16)$$

The male and female scores increase at nearly the same slope ($b = 1.0$), with female scores beginning 1.4 points higher than male scores. Male prestige scores explain 94 percent of the variance in female prestige scores. However, the relationship between the Bose index scores for men and the women's scores developed using Eq. 15 for men looks like this:

$$\text{Female Bose Score Using Male Equation} = 0.74(\text{Male Bose Score}) + 5.1 \quad (17)$$

The slope of the regression line drops to 0.74 and the explained variation declines to 87 percent, while female scores begin 5.1 points higher than male Bose scores. Although women get a higher initial advantage than they do with prestige scores, it is difficult to maintain this lead. Women's low income is responsible for this drop. Thus, the larger raw regression coefficient for income in the original female Bose index [Eq. 3] helps women to compensate for their lower income. If the male formula is instead used for women (Eq. 15), they are robbed of the extra compensation in prestige that they otherwise gain to replace lost income.

Although the beta weight for income clearly varies between men and women as incumbents, these differences are not inherent to the gender of the employee per se. They are the result of the income differential between men and women. If women are assumed to have the same income as men and retain their current educational levels, income becomes equally important (or has the same regression coefficient) in predicting Bose scores for both groups. In fact, it appears that the predictive formulas would be similar if male and female income distributions were also similar.

CONCLUSION

The original NORC scores are similar to the no incumbent scores derived in this study. However, because they were developed from a job sample that underrepresented women's traditional jobs and were presented to respondents in a context implying a male incumbent, NORC scores have a different status distribution than do the no incumbent ones.

Duncan's SEI scores have a similar problem. However, they are even more problematic for women because they were developed using data on male employees. When Duncan's process is replicated using female and male data separately, somewhat different results are obtained for each gender.

Women's no and mixed incumbent prestige scores tend to start lower than do men's scores, and less variance is explained in them by income and education. (The exceptional case is for women in men's jobs.) For both genders, education explains more variance in prestige than does income, and the standardized education regression coefficient is about the same. However, the income contribution to female mixed and no incumbent prestige is less than for males. That is, because women's income curve is generally flat, income is less related to the standing of women's jobs than it is for men.

These differences suggest the importance of using two separate equations for women and men to predict prestige for any given occupation. When the equations relating income and education to mixed incumbent prestige are used to project separate female and male status scores, the resulting scales have been called the "Bose index" by the NLS. The NLS developed such scores for the detailed 1960 census categories, and we so do here for 1970 and 1980. First, the relationship of incumbent prestige to income and education for each year is found for the 108 labor force jobs rated in this study. Then those regression equations are used to project Bose scores for men and women in each detailed occupational census category. These scores can be easily used by mobility researchers. If income and education data are available for respondents, a researcher may also use the predictive equations separately for each gender incumbent, as provided. However, in no case should the male predictive equation be used for women, because the resulting scores will underestimate women's prestige.

The differences in the contribution of income and education to female and male scores appear to be a function of the separate labor markets, or at least of the disparate incomes, of women and men. Even women in traditional men's jobs have different income contributions to prestige than do their sisters in traditional women's jobs. Only when male income levels are attributed to women do the male/female regression coefficients become nearly identical. Therefore, the different predictive equations for women's and men's prestige are not immutably attached to the gender of the job incumbent. Increased income equity should result in similar prestige prediction equations.

6

CONSENSUS AMONG INDIVIDUALS AND IN OCCUPATIONAL RATINGS

In previous chapters we have concentrated on variations in the overall prestige ratings that are associated with characteristics of the occupations, the treatment variables, and the respondents. In Chapter 3, it was shown that both implicit gender (percentage female in a job) and explicit gender (the actual incumbent) interact with the respondent's gender to create the final incumbent occupational prestige score. In fact, the differences caused by sex of respondent are greater than those caused by socioeconomic status.

In this chapter, we instead concentrate on consensus both among individuals within each treatment and at the level of the occupation. Even though there is much agreement on the mean occupational ratings, some individuals more accurately perceive the normative structure of the occupational hierarchy than do others. This analysis will explore who such people are and what characteristics are associated with their accurate perception of job prestige.

On the other hand, regardless of individual perceptions, the prestige of some occupations exhibits more variation than do others: There are jobs, like sociologist, which are not well understood by the public, as well as jobs that are understood, such as housewife, but about which there is less agreement. Furthermore, Powell and Jacobs (1983) argue that there is less consensus on jobs with female incumbents than on occupations with male or no incumbents specified. They find this disagreement over female incumbents in women's and men's jobs and among both male and female raters. Since their sample was a college one, we were interested to test if these findings are replicated in our household sample.

Thus, the task of this chapter is to explore the cause and degree of agreement within each respondent/incumbent treatment and around each occupation. High degrees of consensus will illustrate the relative stability of the ratings, whereas lower degrees may suggest a flux in the gendered prestige of a particular occupation or for particular incumbents.

INDIVIDUAL'S CONSENSUS WITH THE GROUP

To discover the characteristics that increase the probability of agreement with the ratings of others, we develop a measure of the relationship between an individual's occupational rankings and the average rankings given for the experimental treatment (incumbent type) the respondent received. The variable used to measure this relationship is the Pearson correlation coefficient (R). It is derived by matching a respondent's ratings of each job with the average rating of that job by other women or men (as appropriate) in the respondent's treatment group. The correlation is based on labor force jobs, since the amount of dissension over the status of housewife is atypical of other occupations and has been examined in Chapter 4.

At this stage of the analysis, individual variation due to respondent's gender or incumbents rated is mitigated because the comparison is with persons in the same treatment. Thus, there are high correlations between individual ratings and the treatment means. In the household sample, the average correlation is 0.77 with a standard deviation of 0.15, whereas in the college sample the correlation is 0.85 with a standard deviation of 0.09. As suggested by Powell and Jacobs (1983), college students exhibit both a higher average agreement with the norm and a smaller range of disagreement than do householders. This is not surprising since the students came from a more homogeneous background than did the population sample, and because those with higher education also tend to show more accurate perceptions of the norms.

Table 6-1 indicates that within each sample, male and female respondents are equally likely to agree with members of their own gender on the ratings accorded. Comparing columns 1 and 2, it is clear that the correlations are frequently identical and that the maximum correlation difference is 0.03.

There is slightly more difference among the treatments. In each sample, the no incumbent treatment has an overall correlation value different by about 0.04 from the three incumbent treatments. The householders show more agreement about no incumbent prestige than with incumbents present, whereas the college students show more agreement when incumbents are present. However, in neither case is there any difference in the level of agreement between male and female incumbents, as was found by Powell and Jacobs (1983).

TABLE 6-1

Average Correlations of Individual Ratings with Treatment Means (by Sample)

	Mean Correlation		
Treatment	(1) Female Respondents	(2) Male Respondents	(3) All Respondents
Household sample (n = 197)			
Female incumbents only	0.76	0.76	0.76
Male incumbents only	0.76	0.78	0.77
No incumbents	0.81	0.78	0.80
Mixed-gender incumbents	0.77	0.77	0.77
Overall	—	—	0.77
College sample (n = 195)			
Female incumbents only	0.86	0.84	0.85
Male incumbents only	0.84	0.86	0.85
No incumbents	0.82	0.81	0.82
Mixed-gender incumbents	0.86	0.86	0.86
Overall	—	—	0.85

In the college sample, all of the 195 correlations contributing to the mean values in Table 6-1 are positive and above 0.35. In the household sample, only 4 of the 197 correlations are negative. Two of the negative values are near zero, indicating a random sorting of the occupations, and the other two are quite large (-0.76 and -0.84), suggesting either that the respondent reversed the scale or that there was interviewer error in placing the sorted cards in the appropriate envelope.

All of the correlations are slightly artifactual because they are derived from a case base of about 20 persons within each treatment. Each respondent therefore contributes one-twentieth of the mean to which she or he is compared. This explains why the standard deviation around the mean correlation is relatively small. The low variation in the dependent variable will make it difficult for any individual characteristic to explain statistically the variation in degree of agreement with the norm. Because of this problem, R^2 was chosen as the dependent variable, to slightly increase the variation. The standard deviation of R^2 is 0.18 in the household sample and 0.11 in the college group. Under these conditions of relatively low variation, those individual characteristics that are significant become even more interesting.

Once individuals are characterized by this measure (R^2) of normative perception or agreement with others, they are then characterized by their demographic and attitudinal attributes.

The demographic variables include gender of respondent, education level, age, family prestige, income tract of residence (for householders), race (for college students), and whether or not the respondent's mother was employed.

Attitudinal measures are derived from questionnaire items. Many of these items do not distinguish among respondents, since all agreed on one answer. However, at least two questions on the subject of occupational segregation elicited a diversity of response, particularly when they focused on the status of women in "men's jobs."

To determine the effect of these individual level variables on consensus with the group, R^2 values are regressed on the demographic and attitudinal characteristics of the respondents, separately for each sample. The results of these regressions indicate which traits are associated with the mean prestige ratings or which subgroups of respondents most accurately perceive the normative value given to jobs. Since gender of respondent was held constant for the correlations and R^2 values, the regression results do not indicate if women or men hold more accurate views of societal consensus. However, it is possible to determine if men or women are more likely to agree with members of their own gender.

Initial regressions (not shown) indicated that most demographic and attitudinal variables do not significantly affect the value of R^2. Thus, a second set of regressions that included only the five most important independent variables from the initial runs were carried out. The results of these latter analyses are presented for the household sample in Table 6-2 and for the college respondents in Table 6-3.

Only two variables contribute significantly to the regression for the household sample: level of education and attitude toward a woman holding a man's job. The more education respondents have, the more likely they will accurately perceive how the occupations are rated overall. This finding is parallel to the higher correlation found for the college group. It also is intuitively sensible, since education is a form of socialization into societal norms.

The second significant individual characteristic is an attitude measure derived from the responses to the item:

> Sometimes a woman will take a job that is usually held by men, such as TV repairman or typesetter. Do

TABLE 6-2

Regression of Individual R^2 Values on Selected Individual Characteristics[a] (Household Sample)

Individual Characteristic	Standardized Beta Coefficient
Educational attainment (in years)	0.40*
Status of a woman in a man's job (1 = female equality; 0 = female lower status)	0.24*
Census tract (1 = lowest-income tracts . . . 3 = highest-income tracts)	-0.11
Men and women should not have separate types of jobs (1 = agree; 0 = disagree)	0.08
Respondent's social status (NORC score given to occupation of respondent or spouse)	-0.10
R	0.446*
R^2	0.199*

n = 197. NORC, National Opinion Research Center.
[a]Dependent variable is R^2 computed for each respondent between respondent's scores and average scores for all other respondents of the same sex in the same treatment.
*Significant at 0.01 or better.

you think that such a person would have equal, higher, or lower social standing than the men in that job?
    1. A woman and a man would have equal status.
    2. The woman would have higher status than the man.
    3. The woman would have lower status than the man.
    4. Do not know.

The predominant answers to this question were either that both genders are equal or that women are rated lower than men. The question was coded with dummy variables such that 1 = female equality and 0 = female lower status. The positive beta coefficient for the variable indicates that those who expect equality are most likely to perceive the structure of the overall ratings. In fact, based on the card sort results, most household respondents do rate men and women in

CONSENSUS IN OCCUPATIONAL RATINGS

those jobs fairly similarly, with differences of only two to three points in favor of female incumbents.

Although not statistically significant, it is interesting to note that both respondent's prestige and income level of census tract contribute negatively to the determination of R^2. This implies that those holding lower-prestige jobs or living in lower-income areas are more likely to perceive the average ratings given to the jobs. Since the majority of occupational titles in the sample are blue-collar ones, these respondents may be most familiar with their status. Thus, both the well educated, with a broad knowledge of jobs, and those likely to be holding similar jobs to the sampled ones best perceive the occupational hierarchy. Presumably, it is those in the middle range who are least likely to perceive the norm accurately.

Table 6-3 presents the results of the regression of R^2 on the individual characteristics of college students. As in the household sample, one demographic and one attitudinal variable each contribute significantly to explaining the correlation of individuals with the average treatment ratings. Race of respondent is associated with high agreement, and it is whites who are the most likely to agree with the average. This result may be attributed to two causes. First, the majority (89 percent) of the sample is white and will naturally present the dominant viewpoint in the statistical sense. However, it also appears that black students have been socialized to view the role of working women in a different manner than have whites. This form of analysis cannot separate out the two interpretations, and both may be true.

Equally as interesting is the importance for the students, as well as for the householders, of the attitudinal variable gauging the status of women in men's jobs. Yet the relationship of this variable to R^2 is opposite that found among householders. Students who expect women to have lower status are more likely to perceive accurately the average prestige of jobs. In the actual card sort task, college respondents do not carry out this pattern: There are relatively few differences in treatment of male and female incumbents, and high-prestige students give additional points to female-dominated jobs. It is possible that the questionnaire item is used by college students to present their image of current society, whereas in the card sort task they are presenting the world as they would like it to be. Perhaps the self-administered format of the college student questionnaire allowed them to be more honest about the world they perceived than did the household interviewer format.

In sum, the raw correlations and the regression analyses indicate that higher education increases agreement on the ratings both within the household sample and among students in contrast to

TABLE 6-3

Regression of Individual R^2 Values on Selected Individual Characteristics[a] (College Sample)

Individual Characteristic	Standardized Beta Coefficient
Race of respondent (0 = black; 1 = other)	0.18*
Status of a woman in a man's job (1 = female equality; 0 = female has lower status)	-0.18*
Age (in years)	0.15
Sex (1 = female; 0 = male)	0.09
Mother of respondent held job (1 = mother worked; 0 = mother did not work)	-0.07
R	0.303*
R^2	0.092*

n = 195.

[a]Dependent variable is R^2 computed for each respondent between respondent's scores and average scores for all other respondents of the same sex in the same treatment.

*Significant at 0.01 or better.

the householders: Those with higher education are more likely to perceive the average prestige of a job. Attitudes toward women holding men's jobs are also a major determinant, in both samples, of agreement with the average occupational prestige rating within a treatment. However, attitudes function differently in each sample. Among the householders, those who feel women and men would be treated equally agree with the normative ratings, whereas among the students, those who feel women would be accorded less status are most likely to agree with the average occupational rating.

Turning to gender features, male and female respondents are equally likely to agree with those of their own gender, and incumbent's gender does not change the level of consensus on prestige. However, absence of an incumbent does increase agreement in the household sample and decrease consensus among students.

Although not statistically significant, socioeconomic background behaves similarly in each sample, with lower-socioeconomic status respondents more likely to perceive the normative ranking.

Thus, on the whole, there is considerable consensus among individuals in their ratings of gendered prestige, with education and attitudes toward traditional roles serving as the major determinants of concurrence with the average rating.

VARIATION IN CONSENSUS ON OCCUPATIONS

It is possible for respondents to show high levels of agreement with each other and still to hold collectively varying degrees of consensus across the sampled occupations. Variation around mean occupational prestige scores can be caused by differential public understanding of jobs or by genuine disagreement among subpopulations (such as men versus women or middle-class versus working-class people) as to the rankings of jobs. Further, Powell and Jacobs (1983) have argued that there is also a general disagreement about the relative ranking of women incumbents in any occupation. They use their findings to suggest that the applicability of prestige scores to women is therefore problematic. Since the analysis of Powell and Jacobs is based upon a college sample in which one would expect high consensus, it is of considerable interest to determine if such variation is also found in the ratings of our more heterogeneous householder sample.

Therefore, Table 6-4 presents the standard deviations around the mean prestige ratings given by the Baltimore household respondents to each of the 108 labor force occupations sampled. The standard deviations are shown separately for each incumbent treatment. Columns 1 and 2 are from the treatments with a single-gender incumbent, female and male, respectively. Columns 4 and 5 are for the female and male incumbents when rated in a mixed incumbent format. Finally, column 3 provides a comparison base with the deviations around the no incumbent prestige scores.

The variation within each whole treatment is quite similar, ranging from 30.3 to 30.7. However, more differentiation is found when the mean of the standard deviations is examined. The single-gender treatments seem to reflect the pattern suggested by Powell and Jacobs (1983): The average deviation for female incumbent jobs is 24.2, whereas the figure is only 21.6 for men. Further, the standard deviation of female incumbent scores is greater (although not always statistically) than that for male incumbents in 68 percent of the cases. Yet, this difference is not maintained in the mixed incumbent treatments where male and female incumbent jobs have similar mean standard deviations (21.3 and 21.2, respectively), and where male standard deviations are greater than the female ones for 55 percent of the 108 occupations.

TABLE 6-4

Standard Deviations for Mean Occupational Prestige Ratings of Household Sample (by Incumbent's Gender) — Labor Force Jobs Only[a]

No./Occupation	Single-Gender Incumbents		(3) No Incumbent	Mixed-Gender Incumbents	
	(1) Female	(2) Male		(4) Female	(5) Male
Total treatment	30.7	30.6	30.3	30.3	30.5
1. Box packer	24.2	16.7	17.0	17.5	16.0
2. Fruit harvester (family)	29.8	23.6	23.0	22.0	28.8
3. Assembly line supervisor (manufacturing)	22.5	25.0	19.5	19.8	20.3
4. Fireman, boiler room	26.2	27.5	20.1	21.7	25.2
5. Landscape gardener	27.1	28.6	23.1	29.0	19.6
6. Beautician	24.3	22.3	19.8	20.5	22.4
7. Delivery truck driver	23.7	19.1	21.2	20.8	19.6
8. Saladmaker in a hotel	24.1	19.6	17.9	16.9	22.6
9. Electrical engineer	24.8	22.6	15.6	20.1	20.8
10. Florist	26.3	25.2	22.8	24.3	23.3
11. Stenographer	17.8	20.7	18.2	19.6	22.9
12. Practical nurse	22.6	25.7	19.4	20.3	17.8
13. Garbage collector	26.3	18.9	23.7	25.9	25.1
14. Circulation director of a newspaper	21.8	27.8	24.4	23.8	25.6
15. Metal container maker	25.3	19.9	19.0	20.2	22.3

16. Locomotive engineer	24.8	21.5	19.8	23.6	24.9
17. Vegetable grader	26.0	18.4	22.2	16.9	24.5
18. Flour miller	24.0	19.1	22.1	19.4	19.3
19. Electric wire winder	26.7	24.3	19.5	21.7	22.7
20. Short-order cook	24.4	15.2	18.6	20.0	26.2
21. Stockbroker	25.2	28.3	26.3	22.1	19.6
22. Post office clerk	23.6	20.3	20.8	24.0	21.8
23. Carpenter	25.4	22.0	19.4	24.1	23.4
24. Wholesale salesperson	21.5	20.0	20.5	20.6	16.6
25. Tool machinist	18.5	26.4	23.0	25.0	21.7
26. Keypunch operator	23.3	23.5	21.0	23.3	20.5
27. Shirtmaker, manufacturing	22.7	19.4	17.9	17.5	20.9
28. Bookkeeper	17.7	21.4	20.3	23.2	24.1
29. Chambermaid/bedmaker	22.2	20.3	14.3	16.0	19.7
30. Chiropractor	30.4	24.6	23.0	21.5	23.9
31. High school teacher	18.6	21.7	22.9	21.5	24.3
32. Yarn washer	27.3	13.1	11.6	16.0	13.6
33. Social worker	22.8	26.5	25.7	25.6	26.1
34. File clerk	21.7	24.5	18.1	20.0	20.3
35. Warehouse clerk	26.3	22.7	14.1	19.2	19.2
36. Dental assistant	21.2	23.4	20.6	18.3	22.0
37. Administrative assistant	20.3	21.9	20.3	16.8	23.1
38. Hotel manager	23.7	22.1	19.3	20.2	18.1
39. Office secretary	21.2	20.4	20.4	15.9	20.8
40. Janitor	23.6	9.8	17.4	15.8	23.5

(continued)

TABLE 6-4 (continued)

Occupation	Single-Gender Incumbents		No Incumbent	Mixed-Gender Incumbents	
	(1) Female	(2) Male	(3)	(4) Female	(5) Male
41. Building construction contractor	20.6	19.8	19.3	16.1	16.7
42. City superintendent of schools	19.3	15.9	16.8	17.5	23.9
43. Factory owner, 2,000 workers	29.5	21.3	25.1	18.1	20.3
44. Blacksmith	23.2	23.7	23.0	22.8	25.1
45. Warehouse supervisor	21.8	25.0	23.4	21.5	19.0
46. Coal miner	29.5	19.9	23.4	25.8	24.4
47. Floor finisher	25.6	20.8	19.1	19.8	24.2
48. Cotton farmer	24.7	19.0	28.2	24.8	26.2
49. Butcher (shop)	24.6	22.1	21.0	19.4	21.2
50. Babysitter	29.2	21.4	21.2	21.2	22.4
51. Assembly line worker	24.9	19.5	21.7	17.9	27.3
52. Laundry worker	24.8	19.5	17.2	20.4	21.7
53. Police officer	26.1	21.5	22.1	24.6	23.5
54. Welder	26.7	23.2	21.0	25.3	21.3
55. Advertising executive	23.8	27.1	21.0	16.9	26.4
56. Sociologist	25.8	29.3	24.9	24.5	21.1
57. Private secretary	24.3	23.1	19.1	21.1	17.0
58. Feed grinder	26.2	19.4	16.9	17.5	15.6
60. Waitress/Waiter	26.2	18.0	16.8	22.4	20.0
61. Housekeeper	27.8	26.6	27.4	22.8	26.3

62. Car dealer	24.0	25.0	20.4	24.4	21.9
63. Mayor	22.9	7.6	16.4	17.8	18.7
64. Boardinghouse keeper	28.0	22.7	17.2	22.2	23.9
65. Ragpicker	22.1	13.4	10.6	12.4	17.9
66. Cashier	23.9	23.6	22.5	25.7	20.2
67. Bookbinder	26.0	22.3	17.4	21.8	22.3
68. Stock clerk	23.2	23.6	18.8	26.1	18.3
69. Lawyer	21.9	10.8	19.5	10.9	16.4
70. Pastry chef in a restaurant	24.8	27.2	20.8	23.3	19.4
71. Electrician	23.1	24.7	19.2	21.8	22.3
72. Supervisor of telephone operators	25.4	21.3	21.0	27.0	17.2
73. Manager, supermarket	24.8	22.0	21.6	19.1	17.9
74. Office manager	24.0	21.9	17.4	18.2	19.7
75. Typist	21.6	18.1	20.6	19.2	18.3
76. Shoe salesperson (store)	23.9	19.1	22.2	22.5	19.6
77. Insurance agent	21.8	22.6	19.2	18.9	23.9
78. Powerhouse engineer	26.1	23.8	23.3	20.5	23.7
79. College professor	18.6	19.2	11.5	16.2	19.4
80. Piano tuner	23.4	23.5	20.3	22.7	20.2
81. Truck driver	25.9	23.8	20.1	23.4	23.8
82. Parking lot attendant	24.5	17.5	12.3	20.2	15.6
83. Washing machine repairman	23.7	21.9	20.4	22.1	19.0
84. Auto refinisher	23.7	23.4	21.3	20.4	15.8
85. Physician	23.6	10.7	10.5	19.9	11.5
86. Maid (F)/Household dayworker (M)	26.1	14.8	13.3	24.5	21.4
87. Floor supervisor in a hospital	25.2	23.6	22.7	19.6	24.9

(continued)

TABLE 6-4 (continued)

Occupation	Single-Gender Incumbents		(3) No Incumbent	Mixed-Gender Incumbents	
	(1) Female	(2) Male		(4) Female	(5) Male
88. Bellhop	27.1	16.2	11.7	23.8	11.9
89. Textile machine operator	27.2	22.6	17.8	18.8	17.9
90. Architect	19.2	18.5	15.1	23.9	15.0
91. Hospital lab technician	22.0	24.9	22.6	23.8	21.9
92. Dress cutter	25.4	25.3	19.1	23.8	17.7
93. Telephone operator	22.3	18.9	23.1	24.1	23.1
94. Hospital aide	27.4	26.9	26.2	26.6	24.3
95. Accountant	20.7	21.1	16.0	19.4	19.6
96. Rubber mixer	25.4	20.9	14.8	18.6	25.5
97. Registered nurse	22.6	23.0	17.4	24.5	18.3
98. Plumber	21.2	22.4	19.1	21.8	27.0
99. Factory manager, 2,000 workers	28.4	19.9	24.6	26.2	21.4
100. Typesetter	22.5	23.0	21.5	22.2	20.7
101. House painter	25.4	18.5	20.0	20.2	20.2
103. Shoe repair person	25.3	20.5	22.5	22.8	19.0
104. Carhop	26.5	19.3	13.6	21.7	17.0
105. Artist	28.6	31.7	30.4	29.3	28.5
106. Grade school teacher	26.3	27.4	23.4	21.6	22.6

107. Auto mechanic	24.4	23.7	19.2	21.9	23.1
108. Hairdresser	21.3	23.4	21.2	22.1	21.0
109. Inspector, manufacturing	17.2	21.1	20.4	13.5	23.1
110. Cattle driver working for own family	26.4	25.4	25.6	24.3	26.2
Mean of standard deviations	24.2	21.6	20.0	21.2	21.3

[a]Occupations no. 59 (Housewife/househusband) and no. 102 (Person on welfare) are excluded from this analysis.

It seems that presenting respondents with an all female incumbent labor force increases the amount of variation in the job ratings, but that presentation in a mixed labor force context increases consensus and provides a good frame of reference for respondents. An atypical work force may exacerbate incumbent differences just as can an atypical job sample, focused only on sex-stereotyped jobs. Powell and Jacobs used a mixed-gender labor force presentation in one-third of their questionnaires, whereas the remaining respondents rated either men and general prestige or women and general prestige. Since their analysis is presented only by gender of incumbent, it is impossible to know if they too would find equal consensus on male and female incumbents when examining only the mixed-gender treatment.

Because male and female incumbents may have the same mean standard deviation in the mixed-gender treatments, but reveal less consensus concerning people in sex-stereotyped jobs, it is important to examine the variation in prestige for men in stereotypic women's jobs and women in stereotypic men's jobs. In fact, the importance of attitudes in determining agreement on prestige ratings makes an investigation of women in typically male jobs particularly interesting. Further, although women's employment may be accepted by the population in general, it is in the most stereotyped jobs that one would expect the most resistance and therefore the least agreement on prestige.

The ten most male-dominated jobs (1970) in our sample and their respective standard deviations around the mean female and male prestige ratings (mixed incumbent treatment) are as follows:

Job	Female	Male
Floor finisher (1.6% female)	19.8	24.2
Garbage collector (1.6% female)	25.9	25.1
Electrical engineer (1.6% female)	20.1	20.8
Building construction contractor (1.5% female)	16.1	16.7
Truck driver (1.4% female)	23.4	23.8
Powerhouse engineer (1.4% female)	20.5	23.7
Auto mechanic (1.3% female)	21.9	23.1
Carpenter (1.3% female)	24.1	23.4
Plumber (1.0% female)	21.8	27.0
Locomotive engineer (0.7% female)	23.6	24.9
Mean standard deviation	21.7	21.5

Surprisingly, the mean standard deviations are nearly identical, and in eight of the ten jobs a slightly greater level of disagreement (larger standard deviation) is exhibited over male incumbent prestige than for female incumbents. Assuming that women's entry into high-income male jobs may be more acceptable than men's entry into traditional, and low-status, female jobs, we turn our attention to the latter.

The ten most female-dominated jobs (1970) in our sample and their respective standard deviations for female and male incumbents (mixed-incumbent treatment) are the following:

Job	Female	Male
Housekeeper (98.5% female)	22.8	26.3
Dental assistant (97.8% female)	18.3	22.0
Private secretary (97.6% female)	21.1	17.0
Office secretary (97.6% female)	15.9	20.8
Babysitter (97.5% female)	21.2	22.4
Registered nurse (97.3% female)	24.5	18.3
Hospital floor supervisor (97.3% female)	19.6	24.9
Practical nurse (96.4% female)	20.3	17.8
Maid/dayworker (96.0% female)	24.5	21.4
Dress cutter (95.1% female)	23.8	17.7
Mean standard deviation	21.2	20.9

The average standard deviation is slightly lower among the female-dominated jobs than among the male ones, and once again the mean consensus on male and female incumbents is fairly similar. In this case, five of the jobs reveal more consensus with female incumbents and the other five show more agreement with male incumbents. Thus, the level of consensus on men in women's jobs, women in men's jobs, and persons in sex-stereotypical jobs is about the same, with standard deviations ranging from 20.9 to only 21.7.

What are the jobs on which there is dissension? Among almost all incumbents there is the least agreement on the role of artist, and there is frequently confusion exhibited in the ratings of farm occupations such as fruit harvester, cattle driver, cotton farmer, and even landscape gardener. For women incumbents, some traditional (such as cashier with a standard deviation of 25.7, hospital aide 26.6, social worker 25.6, and telephone operator supervisor 27.0) and some nontraditional (stock clerk 26.1, coal miner 25.8, garbage collector 25.9, and factory manager 26.2) jobs reflect a lack of agreement. Similarly for men, some male (such as short-order cook with a standard deviation of 26.2, assembly line worker 27.2, plumber 27.0, and advertising executive 26.4) and some typically female (housekeeper 26.3 and social worker 26.0) roles show limited consensus. These disagreements may be one result of changing roles, which equally affect women and men as job incumbents.

In sum, in a mixed-gender labor force, there are equal degrees of consensus on the prestige of female and male incumbents. This is true in both traditionally gender-stereotyped jobs as well as in nontraditional jobs. While changing roles do cause more confusion over incumbents in certain jobs, the net impact is no greater on women than on men. In fact, the least consensus exists on artistic and agricultural jobs, rather than among traditionally male industrial and typically female service roles.

CONCLUSION

There is considerable consensus on the prestige of occupations with incumbents. Higher education increases the degree of consensus, as does attitude toward women in nontraditional jobs. However, in the actual ratings, women in men's jobs and men in women's jobs exhibit degrees of consensus similar to those in jobs traditional for their gender. There is no more disagreement over the prestige of working women than over that of employed men. The major factor increasing disagreement in the ratings of women is the presentation of occupations to respondents in an all female incumbent rating task, rather than in a context that accurately represents a mixed-gender labor force.

7

SUMMARY AND CONCLUSIONS: GENDER AND JOBS

In the study of social mobility or status attainment, people are often classified according to the occupations they hold. While early stratification research utilized nominal occupational groupings that were used to define social class, the publication of Reiss's <u>Occupations and Social Status</u> (1961), Hodge et al.'s "Occupational Prestige in the United States: 1925-1963" (1965), and Blau and Duncan's <u>The American Occupational Structure</u> (1967) changed the dominant metric for social origins to continuous status scales.

Recent writers now classify these scales into three categories: subjective, objective, and objective based on subjective measures. Prestige is generally considered to fall into the first category because it is based on the repute an occupation has among the general population. Duncan scores are categorized as objective scores that were developed from a basis in the subjective prestige scores, utilizing income and education to project scores for all occupations. Completely "objective" scores are more recent in their development and are based upon the joint distribution of education and income across all jobs.

Although objective scores may be most suitable for studies of income attainment, they are not as useful for status attainment research as are the other two. Most objective scores are based on a forced distribution of one-tenth of all persons within each education and income decile. This does not indicate the class groupings into which jobs fall. However, the summary scores reveal larger percentages of people in the center of the distribution. While prestige is also a continuous measure, without class line demarcations, it and the objective scales based upon it are measured to allow any natural status clustering to occur. Prestige measures also have the advantage of not fluctuating over time, while objective percentile-based measures will vary with the numbers of people holding each job.

In the late 1960s and early 1970s, most researchers assumed that these scales were equally valid for both male and female job incumbents. At the time, this issue seemed less relevant because a woman's mobility was still being measured from her father to her spouse, if it was considered at all. However, the increasing numbers of employed women and of female-headed households, as well as the women's movement, made it impossible to ignore women's independent social mobility and their contribution to household social standing.

The consistent 60 percent income gap between men and women, as well as the existence of gender-segregated labor markets, led to research on the comparative mobility processes of men and women. These studies inevitably led to questioning of the usefulness of social standing scores, constructed from male data, for research on women's employment. However, it has only been in the 1980s that objective status scores were constructed for the total labor force.

On the other hand, no thorough analysis of the impact of gender on occupational prestige had been carried out; and no study simultaneously and systematically investigated the prestige of a wide range of gender-typed jobs, controlling for the effects of gender incumbency and rater characteristics and using a representative population sample. The research reported in this volume, with its primary focus on the impact of gender in the measurement of occupational prestige, fills this gap. The results are useful both because prestige scores have been important in their own right for social mobility studies and because they are the basis for the frequently used Duncan scores. This volume also develops separate Duncan scores for men and women, called the "Bose index" by the NLS, for the detailed 1970 and 1980 census occupations by making use of the relationship between incumbent prestige and the changing distributions of average occupational income and education.

SUMMARY

Conceptually, these new incumbent-based prestige scores are ratings of occupational prestige modified by the gender of the incumbent, rather than those of gender prestige and occupational prestige combined to form a new social standing variable. In fact, it is impossible to measure "pure" occupational prestige because it is inherently confounded with the gender of the incumbent, as implied by the percentage of women or men in any given job, as well as by other characteristics such as presumed income, education, age, and race of

SUMMARY AND CONCLUSIONS

the usual jobholder. The advantage of the methodology used here is that it allows the separation of various gender effects (rater, incumbent, and usual incumbent) from other aspects of prestige.

On the basis of this conceptualization of incumbent prestige, it was predicted that the achieved aspect of occupation would be more important than the ascribed characteristic of gender in the determination of gendered incumbent prestige ratings. Because of the past stability of prestige scores, gendered prestige ratings were expected to exhibit high degrees of consensus and to show little variation according to rater characteristics. On the other hand, because men and women receive very different incomes while holding similar occupations, it was predicted that the regression equations indicating the relationship of incumbent prestige to average occupational income and education would reveal different coefficients for men and women. These differences would not be the result of separate status markets for men and women, but rather could be attributed to separate labor markets.

Previous researchers have studied gender's impact on occupational prestige. However, most have drawn on homogeneous college student samples; used only gender-stereotyped jobs or a small job sample; have not simultaneously rated male, female, and no incumbent prestige; or have not utilized both male and female respondents. Because the methodology used here combined the advantages of survey research with those of controlled experiments, this study was free of many of the shortcomings of prior research.

The resulting design interviewed equal numbers of women and men about the prestige of female and male job incumbents holding a full range of gender-stereotyped and gender-neutral occupations. Jobs without incumbents were rated as a control group for those with incumbents, and several non-labor force alternatives (homemaking, welfare) were included for comparison with paid employment. A random household sample was chosen to obtain a broad class base for the job ratings, but a college student group was also interviewed in order to provide comparisons with this or other studies as a potential predictor of future sex role attitudes, and as a sample that holds age and education relatively constant.

Each respondent was asked to rank a set of 110 positions on a scale from 1 (high) to 9 (low). The jobs were presented on IBM cards with or without an incumbent name that indicated gender. The rating task was followed by questionnaire items probing the respondents' general attitudes toward social standing and particularly toward gender and status. These items were used both as a check on the sorting task and as possible explanations for patterns found in the scores.

The 1-9 ratings given to each card by the respondents were converted into the standard NORC prestige metric ranging from 0 (low) to 100 (high) using the following conversion equation:

Prestige Score = (9 - Rating)12.5,

and the resulting prestige scores are presented in Appendix D for each treatment and sample. The actual no incumbent scores range from 5 for ragpicker to 96 for physician as rated by the householders, with a mean rating of 45.

Both genders rate the female-only incumbent jobs higher than in any other treatment, with an average of 49 prestige points. The occupations also exhibit higher variation around the mean ratings here than in any other treatment. These effects are probably caused by the unusual context of an all female labor force. People are accustomed to thinking of a mixed-gender labor force or of men as major "breadwinners." They seem to feel a need to overcompensate an all female labor force, perhaps as an effect of the women's movement or because women would have to work harder than men to achieve success in all of the fields described by the occupational sample. It should be noted, though, that male respondents use a narrower prestige range (16-86) than do women (11-99) within this treatment. Apparently women in the lower ranks of the job scale are unlikely to be seen as failures, and, as in attribution theory, those at the top are unlikely to be seen as successful by male respondents. However, this effect does not occur in other treatments. The unusual response to an all female incumbent treatment casts doubt on the several gender and prestige studies that utilize only female incumbents.

In the college sample, the descriptive statistics present a different picture. Only the no incumbent treatment receives ratings above the mean. Several of the respondents stated that they ignored gender of the incumbent. In fact, they seem to have differentiated more between presence and absence of incumbent.

Gender differences are more exacerbated when stereotyped jobs are compared. Men's jobs reach a top score of near 98, whereas women's scores reach their maximum at 75-80, nearly 20 points lower. The average no incumbent prestige of men's jobs is 50 and of women's jobs 38 points, as rated by the householders. Among students, the comparable figures are 50 and 41. The mean prestige for women's jobs is about ten points lower than for men's jobs, and the latter also exhibit a broader prestige range. Thus, those who have argued for the importance of women's entry into nontraditional jobs are correct if the goal is status maximization.

The remainder of the analysis of gender and prestige interactions is carried out using multivariate techniques. As expected, the achieved status of the job contributes more to the prediction of incumbent occupational prestige than do any of the gender treatment characteristics separately or combined. All together, 48 and 61 per-

SUMMARY AND CONCLUSIONS 93

cent of the variance in the ratings given to the cards by the household and college groups, respectively, is explained by an equation with occupational, treatment, and respondent characteristics as independent variables. Between 1 and 2.5 percent of the variance in the samples is accounted for by the gender-related variables, with the remainder accounted for by the gender-neutral scores. The gender impacts are statistically significant and may add or subtract one to three prestige points, but occupation remains the prime contributor to the repute an individual can gain through positions held. This does not mean that female and male incumbent prestige are determined in an identical manner.

Many pieces of information are taken into account by the respondents in their ratings, and several of the treatment variables interact with each other. Among householders, female incumbents receive an average of two points more than do males. This outcome is the product of an interaction between gender of incumbent and gender of respondent, wherein men lower the scores of male incumbents and women raise the scores of female incumbents. Women, parallel to respondents in other studies, are upgrading their own occupations, while the cause of male "chivalry" is less clear.

This particular interaction does not prevail among college students who ignore most of the data on gender. Such equity may be a result of their higher education, relative inexperience in the job market, or liberal thought. In fact, their ratings reflect much of the current dominant student ideology, which states that the women's movement of the 1960s and 1970s fought, and won, all the battles over job discrimination and that there is now equal opportunity for those willing to work hard. Regardless of the truth of such an assumption, student ratings reflect this impartiality.

Nonetheless, sex segregation of jobs retains its effect on occupational prestige, influencing women and high-status raters in each sample to accord about two additional points to traditional female jobs. This increase occurs only within women's jobs, and does not influence the relative status of women's jobs vis-à-vis men's occupations. The mean and range of predominantly female jobs remain lower than those for men. The reality of low income in women's jobs prevents them from achieving high incumbent prestige, independently of the job incumbent.

In spite of any differences between male and female respondents, there is considerable consensus on the ratings accorded. A correlation-based measure of the relationship between an individual's and the average occupational rankings, given for the experimental treatment the respondent received, indicates a high degree of correspondence between those individual ratings and the treatment means. In the household sample, the average correlation is 0.77, and among the college students, it is 0.85. College students exhibit both a higher average level of consensus and a smaller range of disagreement than do the householders; and householders show more agreement about no incumbent prestige, whereas students agree more when an incumbent is present.

Some individual respondents more accurately perceive the normative rating structure of the occupational hierarchy than do others. In the household sample, educated respondents are most likely to do so, and in the college sample, white respondents are most likely to agree with the average ratings. Apparently, higher education increases agreement on the ratings both among householders and among college students as a group in contrast to the householders. This is not surprising because education is a form of socialization into society's norms and because the highly educated represent a homogeneous group. White students agree with the norms because most of the respondents are white, and possibly black students perceive a different ordering to the prestige of jobs. However, women and men are equally likely to agree with members of their own gender about the average ratings.

The most interesting variable explaining agreement, and differentiating the two samples, is an attitudinal question on the prestige of women in men's traditional occupations. Household respondents who agree with the normative ratings feel that men and women would be equal in this situation and rank the cards accordingly. College respondents who agree with their normative ratings feel that women would have a lower status. However, this is not actually how the students rate incumbent prestige in the card-sorting task. Either the majority of each sample place a different interpretation upon the questionnaire item, or the college sample members inconsistently expect gender inequality in the attitude item and then actually accord similar ratings in traditional jobs.

It is possible for respondents to show high levels of agreement with each other and still to hold collectively varying degrees of consensus across the sampled labor force occupations. Such variation around the mean occupational prestige scores can be caused by differential understanding or by genuine disagreement as to the ranking of particular jobs. Some researchers (Powell and Jacobs, 1983) have also argued that female incumbents generally cause more dissension than do male incumbents.

However, the greatest impact on consensus does not come from gender-related variables. There is the least agreement on the role of artist, and there is frequent disagreement on the ratings of agricultural occupations. In the industrial and service U.S. economy, it is easy to understand why respondents would be unsure how to rate agricultural work.

SUMMARY AND CONCLUSIONS

On the other hand, there are equal levels of agreement about women and men in gender-stereotyped jobs. While changing roles do cause confusion over incumbents in certain occupations, the net impact is no greater on women than it is on men.

Further, in a mixed-gender labor force, there are equal degrees of consensus on the prestige of female and male incumbents. There is more disagreement over working women than over working men only when incumbents are presented in the context of a single-gender labor force. This suggests that those studies that rank only women in occupations automatically decrease the range of consensus to be found.

It is the non-labor force positions that exhibit the most variation around their mean prestige ratings. A person on welfare is universally rated near the bottom of the prestige scale, but the status of the housewife fluctuates with the experimental treatment and the gender of the rater. The housewife, like the unpaid family farm worker, holds a position valued for its product. The roles are inherently difficult to place on a prestige scale that is related to occupational income.

The householders accord 51 points to a housewife in the no incumbent treatment. This is slightly above the average of 45 points received by all occupations. However, when the housewife is presented to respondents in the context of a mixed-gender labor force, her prestige drops below the average because of an interesting interaction with respondent gender. When there is no incumbent, women rate the housewife at nearly 60 points, whereas men rate the role at 40 points. In the mixed incumbent treatment, women drop their rating to 36, whereas men raise their rating to 50. In the first situation, women appear to rate the housewife highly because of the inherent social value of the task and perhaps because of the motherhood component of the role.

However, when housewifery is compared more directly in the second situation with the roles of both men and women in the labor force, women rate housewife with a standing similar to those jobs that are its closest functional equivalent: kindergarten teacher, chauffeur, laundress, maid, and so forth. In the labor force context, men increase the prestige of housewife. This may be an incentive for women not to compete in the work force with them or to do tasks at home that men would prefer not to share or, more positively, it may reflect a sense that there is greater job control for women at home than there is for many employed workers.

Assuming they are interested in maximizing their status, women can gain more prestige as housewives than they would otherwise obtain in 70 percent of other traditional women's jobs. This may explain why working-class women do not denigrate the role, whereas highly educated women with other status alternatives speak of the role as "only" a housewife.

Housewifery has some positive prestige qualities, but househusbandry is not an equally attractive alternative for men. Househusband, the equivalent of housewife for men, rates well below the average occupation and slightly below the labor force equivalents of the role. The household respondents rate the role at 15 points, whereas the more open-minded students accord 32 points.

To obtain either income or status, men must be in the labor force, whereas women can obtain prestige at home. However, if women were paid in accordance with their prestige (utilizing the 1980 relationship of income, education, and incumbent prestige), housewives would earn approximately $13,000, assuming they had an average education.

For the purposes of mobility studies, the household mixed-gender treatment rating of 44 is the most accurate measure by which to compare the housewife with paid labor force roles. Her lack of paid employment need no longer be considered a status gap. This level of prestige is similar to the average rating the housewife received in Menger's 1932 study and the fifth decile socioeconomic score derived by Dworkin (1981). Thus, the social standing of housewives appears to be stable over time.

In the same experimental treatment, househusband receives a score of 24 from the householders and 27 from the college students. Househusband retains an element of social opprobrium, but it approximates the composite labor force homemaker score of 35. This is also the score projected for a housewife from ratings of family vignettes (Rossi et al., 1974). Future studies of housewife's prestige could help untangle the different ratings homemakers receive under different experimental treatments. The routine and rewarding elements of housework and motherhood could be separately rated in order to determine if the higher no incumbent prestige ratings are due to the latter component; and the status of the supermother, who both holds a fulltime job and does all the housework, might be considered.

Although prestige scores for non-labor force roles have applicability in mobility studies through their direct measurement of social standing, those for labor force jobs have also been used to construct socioeconomic indices, based on the relationship of no incumbent prestige to average occupational income and education. Duncan created the first index of this type, using data on male job incumbents. Such male demographic information does not reflect the income distribution across jobs for women. Further, the sample of jobs selected with which to develop a predictive equation did not include a representative cross sample of female-dominated occupations.

SUMMARY AND CONCLUSIONS

Because of these problems with Duncan's index for the study of women's occupational mobility, new separate predictive equations are developed herein by regressing female (male) incumbent prestige on the median education and income of women (men). Although prestige is stable over time and there is no greater disagreement over the ratings of female than male incumbent prestige, the regression coefficients for income and education vary because of the changing distributions of these job attributes. Therefore, the predictive male and female prestige equations are presented for each of three census decades: of 1960, 1970, and 1980, by Eqs. 3 and 4, 5-8, and 9-12, respectively, in Chapter 5. The consistently large raw regression coefficients for female income are clearly a function of the low income, with little variance, that women receive. In all the equations, the intercept for women is also lower than for men. Thus, women tend to start at lower levels of prestige and have difficulty catching up to men.

In 1960, education was a slightly more important determinant of prestige than was income for both genders, but it helped women and men fairly equally. The raw 1960 income coefficients are larger for women than for men, but the standardized ones are not; and, on the whole, income was more important for men than for women in the prediction of prestige. By 1980, income was the more important determinant of prestige for both genders, and in spite of the differing raw regression coefficients, similar standardized coefficients of 0.46 indicate income now equally helps men and women achieve prestige. In this more recent period, it is education that is less helpful to women (beta = 0.39) than it is to men (beta = 0.44). Thus, separate labor markets have helped to produce different prestige determinants over a 20-year period.

When these separate regression equations for incumbent prestige are used to project social standing scores for men and women in each detailed census occupation, the resulting new scale has been labeled the "Bose index." The NLS version of the Bose index for 1960 census occupations is provided in Appendix E. Male and female incumbent scores have also been constructed and presented in Appendix E, for all workers and for year-round workers in the detailed occupations of the 1970 and 1980 census. By looking up an occupation in the census's Alphabetical Index of Industries and Occupations for the appropriate year, a researcher can determine in which detailed category any respondent job may fall. Then, turning to Appendix E, the appropriate Bose index can be found for that detailed category. If education and income data, and not occupation, are available for respondents, the separate equations above can be used to predict social standing. The resulting scores incorporate any gender effects caused by incumbents' or respondents' gender and by percentage female (or male) usually holding that job.

DISCUSSION

On the whole, nonincumbent prestige is a greater determinant of incumbent prestige than is gender. Nonetheless, gender of incumbent and gender of respondent do interact to produce statistically significant positive status increments for women. More importantly, percentage of women or men usually holding a job is strongly related to occupational prestige—not because women in a job lower its status, but rather because there are no female-dominated jobs that fall above a rating of 75. In the middle of the prestige continuum, there is no significant relationship at all between prestige rating and gender.

It is occupational segregation that causes the lower average prestige received by women as a group. Female-dominated jobs have a lower average status than male-dominated ones, as well as the more constricted prestige range already mentioned. This prestige and job segregation is undoubtedly related to the fact that women still earn 60 percent of the median male income.

Other studies of gender and prestige have found more dramatic gender differences in the ratings of incumbents, particularly in gender-stereotyped jobs. However, much of this discrepancy appears to be caused by the methodology of previous studies. Reliance on college student samples will not produce the same results as a random population sample. More importantly, the selection of jobs to be rated must accurately represent the full continuum of men's and women's work. If only gender-stereotyped roles are used, sex differences are exacerbated. If gender-stereotyped jobs are excluded, the effects of percentage female will be masked by the prestige ratings, as in the early NORC scores. If only men or women are used as respondents, some of the interesting variation in non-labor force roles will be lost. Further, if women are used as the only incumbents, the degree of consensus on the ratings will be mitigated.

The prestige scores obtained from this study, the methodology of which systematically controlled all of these problems, are useful in their own right. They are of interest to psychologists and vocational guidance professionals studying attitudes toward employed women and men. Women's studies researchers will be concerned with the effects of occupational segregation on social standing, as well as with the ratings of housewife and househusband. And, of course, status attainment researchers can more fully appreciate the relationship of gender to prestige or make use of the Bose index constructed to provide ratings for women and men over three decades.

SUMMARY AND CONCLUSIONS

Trends in the economy logically lead to ideas for future research on incumbent prestige. The fluctuating contributions of income and education to job standing imply that these interrelationships should be monitored in the next census. In addition, as fewer women remain fulltime housewives, the relative prestige of supermothers (who do both paid and unpaid work fulltime), parttime housewives (who do both roles parttime), and of single women running their own households might be compared. We expect that the relative impact of incumbent and respondent gender may decline as attitudes continue to change, but that the implied incumbent effects of structural occupational segregation will remain.

APPENDIX A

THE QUESTIONNAIRES

HOUSEHOLD
COLLEGE

HOUSEHOLD QUESTIONNAIRE

SIDNEY HOLLANDER ASSOCIATES

Hello, I'm _____ from Sidney Hollander Associates, and we are conducting a survey for the Johns Hopkins Center for Metropolitan Planning and Research. We are making a study of how people in Baltimore think about where different kinds of people stand on on the social ladder. I would like to interview someone in your household.

In this household, I am supposed to interview a (male, female) adult. (IF NOT OBVIOUS) Is there an adult (man, woman) at home now? (IF THERE IS NO ELIGIBLE RESPONDENT, ASK WHEN AN ELIGIBLE IS LIKELY TO BE AT HOME. RECORD THAT INFORMATION, THANK THE PERSON YOU ARE TALKING TO, AND SAY GOODBYE.)

May I talk to that person?
(REPEAT FIRST TWO PIECES OF INFORMATION WHEN YOU FINALLY MEET POTENTIAL RESPONDENT.)

RESPONDENT NUMBER _____

SEX _____

BLOCK NUMBER _____

DECK COLOR _____

INTERVIEWER _____

APPENDIX A

(1) Some people we have talked to agree that there is a definite ladder of social standing in America—that is, that some kinds of people are regarded as being on the top of the social heap and others are regarded as being on the bottom, with different steps between the two extremes. How about your own opinion? Do you believe that there is a definite ladder of social standing in America to which most people would agree?

    1   AGREE

    2   DISAGREE (DO <u>NOT</u> SKIP NEXT QUESTIONS)

    3   DO NOT KNOW   12 ___

(2) In your opinion, is it fair or unfair to have a ladder of social standing like that?

    1   FAIR

    2   UNFAIR

    3   DO NOT KNOW

    4   NOT APPLICABLE   13 ___

(3) What kinds of people generally are on the top of the ladder of social standing?

    _____   14-15 ___

    _____   16-17 ___

    _____   18-19 ___

(4) What kinds of jobs do people with high social standing have?

    _____   20-21 ___

(5) How much education do you think people with high social standing usually have?

    _____   22-23 ___

(6) Do people at the top of the ladder come from any particular nationality or background?

    _____   24-25 ___

(7) What kinds of people are on the bottom of the ladder of social standing?

_____ 26-27 ___

_____ 28-29 ___

_____ 30-31 ___

(8) What kinds of jobs do people on the bottom of the ladder of social standing have?

_____

_____ 32-33 ___

(9) How much education do you think people with low social standing usually have?

_____ 34-35 ___

(10) Do people at the bottom of the social ladder often come from any particular background or nationality?

_____ 34-35 ___

NOW COMES THE CARD-SORTING TASK.

IF YOU ARE USING A DECK OF BLUE CARDS, TURN TO PAGE 4 [106]. THIS DECK HAS ONLY OCCUPATIONS, AND NOT PEOPLE'S NAMES ON THEM.

IF YOU ARE USING A GREEN, YELLOW, OR WHITE DECK, BEGIN THE TASK AS DESCRIBED HERE.

People differ in a lot of ways. We have made up descriptions of different kinds of people. Here is a box with nine different slots in it. (OPEN BOX ON TABLE AND HAND RESPONDENT FIRST CARD IN PACK.) Here is a card with the description of a person.

a. Please put the card in the slot labeled number one if you think that a person like that described on the card would have the highest possible social standing.

b. Put the card in the slot labeled number nine if you think that a person like that would have the lowest possible social standing.

c. If the person would belong somewhere in between, just put the card in the slot that matches the social standing of the person, between one and nine.

APPENDIX A   105

(OBSERVE RESPONDENT'S PLACEMENT OF THE CARD. IF SHE OR HE IS UNCERTAIN AS TO HOW TO PERFORM THE TASK, EXPLAIN IT AGAIN, REMAINING CLOSE TO THE WORDING ABOVE. AFTER THE FIRST CARD IS SUCCESSFULLY PLACED, CONTINUE BELOW.)

d. Here are some more cards (HAND RESPONDENT THE REST OF THE PACK OF CARDS) with descriptions of other kinds of people. Just put them in the slots on the box that match the social standing they would have. Remember that slot number one is the highest standing, and slot number nine is the lowest.

If you want to change your mind about a person, just put it in a different slot.

Some of these people may seem a little unusual to you. Try to place them as best you can.

e. WHEN RESPONDENT HAS COMPLETED PLACING THE ENTIRE DECK OF CARDS, RECORD BELOW <u>ANY SLOTS</u> INTO WHICH THE RESPONDENT HAS PLACED CARDS (USE "X").

___ ___ ___ ___ ___ ___ ___ ___ ___   36-44 ___
 1   2   3   4   5   6   7   8   9

THEN ASK:

f. Would you like to change the place of any of the cards, or place the ones that you were unable to place before? (QUESTION TO R)

ENCOURAGE RESPONDENT TO REVIEW HIS PLACEMENTS.

g. PLACE CARDS IN ENVELOPES ACCORDING TO THE SLOT THEY CAME FROM.

(11) When sorting the cards, what counted more in your decisions—the job or the name of the person?

    1 ONLY THE JOB

    2 MOSTLY THE JOB, AND THE PERSON SOMEWHAT

    3 THE PERSON AND THE JOB COUNTED EVENLY

    4 MOSTLY THE PERSON, AND THE JOB SECONDARILY

    5 ONLY THE NAME OF THE PERSON

    6 NA   45 ___

FOR GREEN, YELLOW, AND WHITE DECKS ONLY:

(12) Would it have helped in sorting people to know if they were married or not?

    1 IT WOULD HELP

    2 IT WOULD MAKE NO DIFFERENCE

    3 IT WOULD MAKE IT HARDER

    4 NA   46 ___

SKIP TO QUESTION 14, NEXT PAGE.

FOR BLUE DECKS, CARRY OUT THE SORTING TASK AS FOLLOWS:

Jobs differ in a lot of ways. We have made up descriptions of different kinds of jobs. Here is a box with nine different slots labeled in it. (OPEN BOX ON TABLE AND HAND RESPONDENT FIRST CARD IN PACK.) Here is a card with the description of a job.

a. Please put the card in the slot labeled number one if you think that a job like that described on the card would have the highest possible social standing.

b. Put the card in the slot labeled number nine if you think that a job like that would have the lowest possible social standing.

c. If the job would belong somewhere in between, just put the card in the slot that matches the social standing of the job, between one and nine.

(OBSERVE RESPONDENT'S PLACEMENT OF THE CARD. IF SHE OR HE IS UNCERTAIN AS TO HOW TO PERFORM THE TASK, EXPLAIN IT AGAIN, REMAINING CLOSE TO THE WORDING ABOVE. AFTER THE FIRST CARD IS SUCCESSFULLY PLACED, CONTINUE BELOW.)

d. Here are some more cards (HAND RESPONDENT THE REST OF THE PACK OF CARDS) with descriptions of other kinds of jobs. Just put them in the slots in the box that match the social standing they would have. Remember that slot number one is the highest social standing, and slot number nine is the lowest.

If you want to change your mind about a job, just put the card in a different box.

Some of these jobs may seem a little unusual to you. Try to place them as best you can.

APPENDIX A 107

e. WHEN RESPONDENT HAS COMPLETED PLACING THE ENTIRE DECK OF CARDS, RECORD BELOW (USE "X") <u>ANY SLOTS</u> INTO WHICH THE RESPONDENT HAS PLACED CARDS.

__ __ __ __ __ __ __ __ __   36-44 __
1   2   3   4   5   6   7   8   9

THEN ASK:

f. Would you like to change the place of any of the cards or place the cards what you were unable to place before? (QUESTION TO R.)

ENCOURAGE RESPONDENT TO REVIEW HIS PLACEMENT OF THE CARDS.

g. PLACE CARDS IN ENVELOPES ACCORDING TO THE SLOT THEY CAME FROM.
UNSORTED CARDS GO IN A SEPARATE ENVELOPE.
BAND ALL OF THE ENVELOPES TOGETHER.

(13) When sorting the cards, did you think of the people holding the jobs as men or as women?

    1 ASSUMED THEY WERE ALL HELD BY <u>MEN</u>

    2 ASSUMED THEY WERE ALL HELD BY <u>WOMEN</u>

    3 ASSUMED THAT THEY COULD BE HELD BY <u>EITHER</u> SEX

    4 DID <u>NOT ASSUME</u> EITHER SEX

    5 <u>DEPENDED ON</u> THE PARTICULAR <u>JOB</u>

    6 NOT APPLICABLE   47 __

CONTINUE ON FROM HERE. ALL QUESTIONS ARE THE SAME FOR <u>ALL</u> COLORS OF <u>DECKS</u>.

(14) Now I would like to ask you some questions about yourself.

    a. In total, how many adults (over 18 years of age) live here in the household with you?

        _____ 48-49 __

    b. How many children live here?

        _____ 50-51 __

    c. How are you related to the head of the household?

        _____ 52-53 __
        (e.g., CHILD, PARENT, SPOUSE)

d. How old are you?

_____ 54-55 ___
(RECORD AGE IN YEARS AT LAST BIRTHDAY)

(15) [Question eliminated]

(16) Are you working, or doing something else at present?

    1 WORKING   (SKIP TO Q. 17)

    2 UNEMPLOYED, BUT LOOKING FOR WORK
       (SKIP TO Q. 19)

    3 ON VACATION, BUT EMPLOYED (SKIP TO Q. 17)

    4 GOING TO SCHOOL   (SKIP TO Q. 19)

    5 RETIRED   (SKIP TO Q. 20)

    6 HOUSEWIFE   (SKIP TO Q. 19)

    7 UNEMPLOYED, NOT LOOKING FOR WORK—
      THIS DOES <u>NOT</u> INCLUDE <u>HOUSEWIFE</u>
      (SKIP TO Q. 19)   59 ___

(17) (IF EMPLOYED) What is your job?

_____

_____ 60-62 ___

(18) (IF EMPLOYED) In what type of business do you work? What does the company do?

_____

_____ 63-64 ___

(19) (IF NOT WORKING AT PRESENT) Have you ever had a job?

    1 YES   (SKIP TO Q. 20)

    2 NO   (SKIP TO Q. 23)

    3 NA   (SKIP TO Q. 23)   65 ___

(20) (IF NOT WORKING AT PRESENT) How long ago was it when you worked?

    _____ (CODE IN MONTHS)   66-67 ___

APPENDIX A   109

(21) (IF NOT WORKING AT PRESENT) What was your
last job?

_____

_____   68-70 ___

(22) (IF NOT WORKING AT PRESENT) In what type of
business did you work? What did the company do?

_____   71-73 ___

(23) Are you married or single? (ASK ONLY IF NOT
OBVIOUS FROM Q. 15)

    1 MARRIED, INCLUDES COMMON LAW

    2 SINGLE (SKIP TO Q. 27)

    3 SEPARATED OR DIVORCED

    4 WIDOWED   74 ___

                                                    2//   1-7 ___

(24) Does (did) your husband (wife) work?

    1 YES   (SKIP TO Q. 25)

    2 NO   (SKIP TO Q. 27)

    3 NA   (SKIP TO Q. 27)   8 ___

(25) What kind of job does (did) he (she) have?

_____

_____   9-11 ___

(26) In what type of business is (was) this? What
does (did) the company do?

_____

_____   12-14 ___

(27) Thinking back to when you were around 16 years
old, did your mother work?

    1 YES   (SKIP TO Q. 28)

    2 NO   (SKIP TO Q. 31)

    3 NA   (SKIP TO Q. 32)   15 ___

(28) What kind of job did she have? _____

_____ 16-18 ___

(29) In what type of business was that? _____

_____ 19-21 ___

(30) In your opinion, did she enjoy her job?

    1 YES

    2 MOST OF THE TIME

    3 SOMETIMES

    4 NOT AT ALL

    5 SHE WORKED BECAUSE SHE HAD TO, AND DID NOT ENJOY IT

    6 NA   22-24 ___

(31) In your opinion, how did your mother feel about the duties of a housewife? (SHOW R CARD WITH RESPONSES)

    1 FELT THAT SHE SHOULD BE DOING SUCH TASKS, AND ENJOYED DOING THESE THINGS FOR THE FAMILY

    2 FELT THAT SHE SHOULD BE DOING SUCH TASKS, BUT WAS NOT VERY INTERESTED IN THEM

    3 FELT THAT SHE SHOULD BE DOING SUCH TASKS, BUT HAD OUTSIDE HELP TO DO THEM

    4 FELT THAT SHE SHOULD BE DOING SUCH TASKS, BUT DISLIKED THEM

    5 FELT THAT SHE SHOULD NOT HAVE TO DO ALL OF THE HOUSEHOLD TASKS, AND RESENTED DOING THEM

    6 FELT THAT SHE SHOULD NOT HAVE TO DO ALL OF THE HOUSEHOLD TASKS, AND HAD OTHER MEMBERS OF THE FAMILY OR HIRED PEOPLE TO HELP DO THE CHORES

    7 NA   25 ___

APPENDIX A   111

(32) What was the last grade you completed in school?

    GRADE _____ DEGREE _____   26-27 ___

    (CODE BOTH THE NUMBER OF YEARS   28-29 ___
    ACTUALLY COMPLETED AS WELL AS THE
    DEGREE. DO NOT INCLUDE POST-HIGH
    SCHOOL VOCATIONAL TRAINING.)

(33) Now I would like to ask a few general questions about social standing.
Generally speaking, do you think that a man and a woman who hold the same job have the same social standing?

    1 YES

    2 NO—THE WOMAN HAS LESS SOCIAL STANDING

    3 NO—THE WOMAN HAS MORE SOCIAL STANDING

    4 IT DEPENDS ON THE JOB

    5 NA   30 ___

(34) Once in a while a woman and a man will have the same job, such as assembly line worker, but they will get different pay. Does this seem fair to you?

    1 YES

    2 NO

    3 DO NOT KNOW   31 ___

(35) It has been said that even if men and women have the same job, women should be paid less because they do not have families to support, and men do. How do you feel about this? Does this seem fair to you?

    1 YES, IT IS FAIR

    2 NO, IT IS NOT FAIR

    3 DO NOT KNOW   32 ___

(36) Sometimes women and men who hold the same job are not paid the same pay, because women are not able to work as hard as men. That is, women are paid less

because they cannot move heavy weights, move fast, and the like. Does this seem fair to you?

    1 YES

    2 NO

    3 DO NOT KNOW   33 ___

(37) Another reason for giving different pay to men and women who do the same job is that men usually have more responsibility or perhaps the more important job on the assembly line. Does this seem to be a good reason to pay people differently?

    1 YES

    2 NO

    3 DO NOT KNOW   34 ___

(38) Very often, men and women will go into different types of jobs. For example, women might become kindergarten teachers and men might become mechanics. There are many arguments for and against such a system. I am going to read several statements about separate jobs for men and women. Please tell me if you agree, disagree, or have mixed feelings about each statement.

    A. Since men and women often have a hard time working with each other, it is easier to have separate types of jobs for men and women.

        1 AGREE

        2 DISAGREE

        3 MIXED FEELINGS

        4 DO NOT KNOW   35 ___

    B. People should feel free to enter any type of job they please.

        1 AGREE

        2 DISAGREE

        3 MIXED FEELINGS

        4 DO NOT KNOW   36 ___

APPENDIX A 113

    C. Women cannot be in every field, because they cannot physically do certain jobs.

        1 AGREE

        2 DISAGREE

        3 MIXED FEELINGS

        4 DO NOT KNOW 37 __

    D. Although people should feel free to take any job, certain jobs are more suited for women because they have hours that fit in with school hours, or because they allow one to stop and have children and then return to them again later.

        1 AGREE

        2 DISAGREE

        3 MIXED FEELINGS

        4 DO NOT KNOW 38 __

    E. People should feel free to enter any job they please, and provisions such as day care centers should be set up to help women enter fields they haven't been able to go into before.

        1 AGREE

        2 DISAGREE

        3 MIXED FEELINGS

        4 DO NOT KNOW 39 __

    F. It makes more sense for men to be in career types of jobs, since in the long run men are more responsible to a job.

        1 AGREE

        2 DISAGREE

        3 MIXED FEELINGS

        4 DO NOT KNOW 40 __

(39) When people go into different sorts of jobs, it means that men often work with men, or women work with women. But sometimes a woman becomes a supervisor over men. Do you think this situation would make

it difficult for the men or the woman to get work done easily? (CIRCLE AS MANY AS APPLY) (SHOW R CARD WITH RESPONSES ON IT)

    1 IT WOULD BE DIFFICULT FOR THE MEN

    2 IT WOULD BE DIFFICULT FOR THE WOMAN SUPERVISOR

    3 IT WOULD BE NO DIFFERENT FROM ANY OTHER SUPERVISOR-WORKER RELATIONSHIP

    4 IT WOULD BE EASIER FOR THE MEN

    5 IT WOULD BE EASIER THAN USUAL FOR THE WOMAN SUPERVISOR

    6 DO NOT KNOW   41-42 ___

(40) Sometimes a man will take a job in a field that is usually made up of women—such as nursing or secretarial work. Do you think such a man would have equal, higher, or lower social standing as a woman in that job?

    1 MAN AND WOMAN WOULD HAVE SAME STATUS (SKIP TO Q. 43)

    2 MAN WOULD HAVE HIGHER STATUS (SKIP TO Q. 41)

    3 MAN WOULD HAVE LOWER STATUS (SKIP TO Q. 42)

    4 DO NOT KNOW   43 ___

(41) Why do you think a man would have more status in that situation?

    1 THE MAN WOULD PROBABLY BE THE SUPERVISOR

    2 OTHER (EXPLAIN) _____

    _____

    3 NA   44 ___

SKIP TO QUESTION 43.

APPENDIX A

(42) Why do you think that a man would have less status in that situation?

    1 IT IS A WOMAN'S JOB

    2 HE COULD EARN MORE MONEY ELSEWHERE

    3 OTHER (EXPLAIN) _____

_____

    4 NA   45 __

(43) Sometimes a woman will take a job that is usually held by men, such as TV repairman or typesetter. Do you think that such a person would have equal, higher, or lower social standing than the men in that job?

    1 A WOMAN AND A MAN WOULD HAVE <u>EQUAL</u> STATUS (SKIP TO Q. 46)

    2 THE WOMAN WOULD HAVE <u>HIGHER</u> STATUS THAN THE MEN (SKIP TO Q. 44)

    3 THE WOMAN WOULD HAVE <u>LOWER</u> STATUS THAN THE MEN (SKIP TO Q. 45)

    4 DO NOT KNOW   46 __

(44) Why do you think the woman would have higher status than the men in that job?

    1 BECAUSE IT IS <u>UNUSUAL</u> FOR A WOMAN TO TAKE A MAN'S JOB

    2 OTHER (EXPLAIN) _____

_____

    3 NA   47 __

SKIP TO QUESTION 46.

(45) Why do you think that the woman would have lower status than the men in that type of job?

    1 THE WOMAN WOULD NEVER HAVE A HIGH-RANKING POSITION IN THAT JOB

    2 OTHER (EXPLAIN) _____

_____

    3 NA   48 __

(46) On the whole, do you think working men have higher social standing than working women?

    1 MEN HAVE HIGHER STANDING
    2 WOMEN HAVE HIGHER STANDING
    3 BOTH HAVE EQUAL STANDING
    4 DO NOT KNOW   49 ___

This is the end of the interview. I'd like to thank you very much for your time and effort. Goodbye.

ADDRESS OF DWELLING UNIT: _____

APPENDIX A

COLLEGE QUESTIONNAIRE

The Johns Hopkins University

Department of Social Relations
Center for Metropolitan Planning and Research

<u>Survey of Baltimore Views on Social Standing</u>

We are making a study of how people in Baltimore think about where different kinds of people stand on the social ladder, or what their status is. Your cooperation in filling out this questionnaire is greatly appreciated.

If you have any questions after the interview, you may contact:

Christine E. Bose
Department of Sociology
Johns Hopkins University
366-3300 ext. 1087

or

Dr. Peter H. Rossi
Department of Sociology and
Center for Metropolitan Planning and Research
366-3300 ext. 1272

YOUR REPLIES ARE CONFIDENTIAL. PLEASE DO <u>NOT</u> SIGN YOUR NAME TO THIS QUESTIONNAIRE.

Office Use Only:

Respondent Number: ___ ___ ___ / ___

School: ___ ___ ___ / _____

Deck: ___ ___

(1) Some people think that there is a definite ladder of social standing or social status in America—that is, some people are regarded as being on the top of the social heap and others are regarded as being on the bottom, with different steps between the two extremes.

Do you believe that there is a definite ladder of social standing in America to which most people would agree? (Circle one)

      1 Yes

      2 No   12 ___

(2) In your opinion, is it fair or unfair to have a ladder of social standing? (Circle one)

      1 Fair

      2 Unfair   13 ___

(3) What kinds of people generally are on the top of the ladder of social standing? (Answer briefly)

      _____

      _____   14-15 ___

(4) What kinds of people are on the bottom of the ladder of social standing? (Answer briefly)

      _____

      _____   16-17 ___

Please stop here and raise your hand to indicate that you are finished with this first part of the questionnaire.

You will be told when to go on to the second part.

APPENDIX A

People and their jobs differ in a lot of ways. We have made up descriptions of different kinds of people and their jobs. One of these descriptions appears on each card of the deck you have been given. You have also been given a box with slots in it; these slots are numbered from "1" to "9."

a. Please put a card in the slot labeled 1 if you think that the person with a job like that described on the card would have the highest possible social standing.

b. Put a card in the slot labeled 9 if you think that the person with a job like that would have the lowest possible social standing.

c. If the description would belong somewhere in between, just put the card in the slot that matches the social standing of the person, somewhere between 1 and 9.

d. If you want to change your mind about a card, just put it in a different slot.

Some of these descriptions may seem a little unusual to you. Try to place them as best you can. Raise your hand if you have any questions.

e. When you are done sorting all the cards in your deck, mark below the slots into which you have placed any cards. (Use an "X")

__ __ __ __ __ __ __ __ __
 1   2   3   4   5   6   7   8   9   18-26 __

Once you have done the sorting task and part e above, continue on with the questionnaire, beginning with question 5 following.

Here are some questions about yourself.

(5) a. What is your sex? (Circle one)

   1 Female

   2 Male   27 __

b. What is your race? (Circle one)

    1 Black (Negro)

    2 White

    3 Other (Oriental, Spanish, American Indian, etc.)   28 ___

c. What is your class in school? (Circle one)

    1 Freshman

    2 Sophomore

    3 Junior

    4 Senior

    5 Graduate

    6 Other   29 ___

d. How old were you at your last birthday?

    __ __ years old   30-31 ___

(6) Are you married or single? (Circle one)

    1 Married

    2 Single

    3 Separated or divorced

    4 Widowed   32 ___

(7) Who is the head of your household? That is, who is the main wage earner? (Circle one)

    1 Yourself

    2 Spouse

    3 Father

    4 Mother

    5 Other   33 ___

(8) a. What <u>job</u> does the <u>head of the household</u> hold? That is, what does he/she do for a living? (If living on Social Security, public assistance, alimony, etc., please indicate this as a job.)

_____

_____   34-36 ___

APPENDIX A

b. In what type of business does the main wage earner work? What does the company or business do?

_____

_____ 37-39 ___

(9) Thinking back to when you were 16 years old, did your mother work? (Circle one)

    1 Yes

    2 No   (Skip to question 11)

    3 Do not know (Skip to question 11)   40 ___

(10) If your mother did work,

  a. What kind of job did she have? _____

_____ 41-43 ___

  b. In what type of business was that? _____

_____ 44-46 ___

  c. In your opinion, did she enjoy her job? (Circle one)

    1 Yes

    2 Most of the time

    3 Sometimes

    4 Not at all

    5 She worked because she had to, and did not enjoy it

    6 Do not know   47 ___

(11) In your opinion, how did or does your mother feel about the duties of a housewife? (Circle one)

    1 Felt that she should be doing such tasks, and enjoyed doing these things for the family

    2 Felt that she should be doing such tasks, but was not very interested in them

    3 Felt that she should be doing such tasks, but had outside help to do them

    4 Felt that she should be doing such tasks, but disliked them

5 Felt that she should not have to do all of the household tasks, and resented doing them

6 Felt that she should not have to do all of the household tasks, and had other members of the family or hired help to aid in the chores

7 Do not know   48 ___

Now here are a few general questions about social standing.

(12) Generally speaking, do you think that a man and a woman who hold the same job have the same social standing? (Circle one)

    1 Yes

    2 No—the woman has less social standing

    3 No—the women has more social standing

    4 It depends on the job   49 ___

(13) Once in a while, a man and a woman will have the same job, such as assembly line worker, but they will get different pay. Does this seem fair to you? (Circle one)

    1 Yes

    2 No

    3 Do not know   50 ___

(14) It has been said that even if men and women have the same job, women should be paid less because they do not have families to support and men do. How do you feel about this? Does this seem fair to you? (Circle one)

    1 Yes, it is fair

    2 No, it is not fair

    3 Do not know   51 ___

(15) Sometimes women and men who hold the same job are not paid the same pay because women are said not to be able to work as hard as men. That is, women are paid less because they cannot move heavy weights, move fast, and the like. Does this seem fair to you? (Circle one)

APPENDIX A

    1 Yes

    2 No

    3 Do not know   52 ___

(16) Another reason for giving different pay to men and women who do the same job is that men usually have more responsibility or perhaps the more important job on the assembly line. Does this seem to be a good reason to pay people differently? (Circle one)

    1 Yes

    2 No

    3 Do not know   53 ___

(17) Very often, men and women will go into different types of jobs. For example, women might become kindergarten teachers and men might become mechanics. There are many arguments for and against such a system. Below are several statements about separate jobs for men and women. Indicate if you agree, disagree, or have mixed feelings about each statement by marking an "X" in the appropriate column.

	Agree	Disagree	Mixed Feelings	Do Not Know	
A. Since men and women often have a hard time working with each other, it is easier to have separate types of jobs for men and women.					54 ___
B. People should feel free to enter any type of job they please.					55 ___
C. Women cannot be in every field, because they cannot physically do certain jobs.					56 ___
D. Although people should feel free to take any job, certain jobs are more suited for women because they have hours that fit in with school hours, or because they allow women to stop and have children and return to work again later.					57 ___
E. People should feel free to enter any job they please, and provisions such as day care centers should be set up					

	Agree	Disagree	Mixed Feelings	Do Not Know	
to help women enter fields they have not been able to go into before.					58 ___
F. It makes more sense for men to be in career types of jobs, since in the long run men are more responsible to a job.					59 ___

(18) When people go into different sorts of jobs, it means that men often work with men, or women work with women. But sometimes a woman becomes a supervisor over men. Do you think this situation would make it difficult for the men or the women to get work done easily? (Circle <u>as many as apply</u>)

    1 It would be difficult for the men

    2 It would be difficult for the woman supervisor

    3 It would be no different from any other supervisor-worker relationship

    4 It would be easier for the men

    5 It would be easier than usual for the woman supervisor

    6 Do not know   60-61 ___

(19) Sometimes a man will take a job in a field that is usually made up of women—such as nursing or secretarial work. Do you think such a man would have equal, higher, or lower social standing as a woman in that job? (Circle one)

    1 Man and woman would have the <u>same</u> status (Go to question 22)

    2 Man would have <u>higher</u> status (Go to question 20)

    3 Man would have <u>lower</u> status (Go to question 21)

    4 Do not know (Go to question 22)   62 ___

(20) Why do you think a man would have more status in the situation described in question 19? (Circle one)

    1 The man would probably be the supervisor

APPENDIX A   125

    2 The man would be paid more

    3 Not applicable

    4 In general, people look up to men

    5 Men are expected to do more

    6 Other (Explain) _____ 63 ___

Now go to question 22.

(21) Why do you think that a man would have less status in the situation described in question 19? (Circle one)

    1 It is a woman's job

    2 He could earn more money elsewhere

    3 The man is looking for an easy job

    4 Other (Explain) _____ 64 ___

(22) Sometimes a woman will take a job that is usually held by men, such as TV repairman or typesetter. Do you think that such a person would have equal, higher, or lower social standing than the men in that job?
(Circle one)

    1 A woman and a man would have equal status
       (Go to question 25)

    2 The woman would have higher status than the man
       (Go to question 23)

    3 The woman would have lower status than the man
       (Go to question 24)

    4 Do not know (Go to question 25)   65 ___

(23) Why do you think that the woman described in question 22 would have higher status than the men in that job? (Circle one)

    1 Because it is unusual for a woman to take a man's job

    2 Other (Explain) _____

       _____ 66 ___

Now go to question 25.

(24) Why do you think that the woman described in question 22 would have lower status than the men in that type of job? (Circle one)

    1 The woman would never have a high-ranking position in that job

    2 People prefer men to do these types of jobs

    3 Not applicable

    4 People do not believe women are capable of doing these jobs

    5 Other (Explain) _____

    _____   67 ___

(25) On the average, do you think that men who work have a higher social standing than do women who work? (Circle one)

    1 Men have higher standing

    2 Women have higher standing

    3 Both have equal standing

    4 Do not know   68 ___

After finishing the questionnaire, please fold it in half and place it in the sorting box. Cover the box. It should have the sorted cards and the questionnaire in it.

This is the end of the interview. Thank you very much for your time and effort.

APPENDIX B

THE OCCUPATIONAL SAMPLE AND SAMPLING METHOD

Key[a]	Occupational Title[b]	Detailed 1960 Census Category from Which Occupation Drawn[c]	Source Distribution[d]	Percentage Female in Occupation (1970)[e]	Rank Order for Percentage Female[f]	Estimates of Prestige for Occupation[g]
95	Accountant	000—Accountant	0	26.0	53	56.7
37	Administrative assistant	370—Clerks, not elsewhere classified	1	42.8	42	36.2
55	Advertising executive	290—Managers, officials, and proprietors, not elsewhere classified, business services	0			
90	Architect	013—Architect	9	15.7	60	59.8
105	Artist	014—Artists	0	3.5	85	70.5
3	Assembly line supervisor in a manufacturing plant	430—Foreman, not elsewhere classified	1	35.9	47	57.0
51	Assembly line worker	631—Assemblers	1	8.0	74	45.1
107	Auto mechanic	472—Auto mechanics	0	48.1	38	27.1
84	Automobile refinisher	694—Painters	0	1.3	105	36.7
50	Babysitter	801—Babysitter	1	14.4	64	29.0
				97.5	5	23.2

128

6	Beautician	s—Sales, not elsewhere classified, retail	1	90.1	17	33.2
88	Bellhop	890—Service workers, not elsewhere classified	0	2.5	92	14.4
44	Blacksmith	402—Blacksmith	0	2.4	93	35.5
64	Boardinghouse keeper	821—Boardinghouse keeper	1	71.6	29	22.1
67	Bookbinder	775—Operatives, printing & publishing	1	57.1	35	31.3
28	Bookkeeper	310—Bookkeeper	1	81.9	25	47.6
1	Box packer	693—Packers & wrappers	1	60.9	34	19.4
41	Building construction contractor	290—Managers, officials, and proprietors, not elsewhere classified, construction	0	1.5	102	54.9
49	Butcher in a shop	675—Meat cutter	0	10.4	68	32.1
62	Car dealer	290—Managers, officials, and proprietors, not elsewhere classified, retail	0	2.2	94	43.5

Key[a]	Occupational Title[b]	Detailed 1960 Census Category from which Occupation Drawn[c]	Source Distribution[d]	Percentage Female in Occupation (1970)[e]	Rank Order for Percentage Female[f]	Estimates of Prestige for Occupation[g]
104	Carhop	875—Waiters	0	89.0	19	20.3
23	Carpenter	411—Carpenter	0	1.3	106	42.5
66	Cashier	312—Cashier	1	83.7	23	30.9
110	Cattledriver working for own family	903—Unpaid family farm worker	0	40.1	43	21.4
30	Chiropractor	022—Chiropractor	1	8.2	72	60.0
14	Circulation director of a newspaper	290—Managers, officials, and proprietors, not elsewhere classified, manufacturing	0	3.5	87	60.5
42	City superintendent of schools	183—Secondary school teacher	1	27.1	52	67.4
46	Coal miner	685—Mine operatives	0	2.1	96	25.2
79	College professor	060—College professor	9	28.3	50	78.3
48	Cotton farmer	200—Farm owners	1	4.9	80	40.7
7	Delivery truck driver	650—Deliverymen	0	3.1	90	28.0

36	Dental assistant	303—Physician's attendants	1	97.8	2	47.8
92	Dress cutter	775—Operative, apparel	1	95.1	10	25.8
19	Electric wire winder	775—Operative, electric machinery	1	50.9	37	38.6
9	Electrical engineer	083—Electrical engineer	0	1.6	101	69.4
71	Electrician	421—Electricians	0	1.8	98	49.2
58	Feed grinder	775—Operatives, wholesale & retail	0	28.0	51	25.9
34	File clerk	320—File clerk	1	81.9	24	30.3
4	Fireman in a boiler room	712—Stationary fireman	0	5.1	78	32.5
47	Floor finisher	495—Painters, construction	0	1.6	99	29.8
87	Floor supervisor in a hospital	150—Professional nurses	1	97.3	7	61.5
10	Florist	290—Managers, officials, and proprietors, not elsewhere classified, retail	1	19.5	57	50.3

Key[a]	Occupational Title[b]	Detailed 1960 Census Category from Which Occupation Drawn[c]	Source Distribution[d]	Percentage Female in Occupation (1970)[e]	Rank Order for Percentage Female[f]	Estimates of Prestige for Occupation[g]
18	Flour miller	490—Millers	0	2.2	95	25.2
2	Fruit harvester, working for own family	903—Unpaid farm workers	1	40.1	44	21.4
13	Garbage collector	985—Laborers, not elsewhere classified	0	1.6	100	12.6
106	Grade school teacher	182—Elementary school teachers	1	85.7	21	60.1
108	Hairdresser	843—Hairdressers	1	90.1	16	33.2
31	High school teacher	183—Secondary school teacher	1	46.9	41	63.1
94	Hospital aide	810—Hospital attendants	1	84.8	22	36.3
91	Hospital lab technician	185—Medical technicians	1	71.9	28	61.0
29	Hotel chambermaid (F)/ Hotel bedmaker (M)	823—Maids	1	94.8	11	13.6

38	Hotel manager	290—Managers, officials, and proprietors, not elsewhere classified, personal service	0		
61	Housekeeper	802—Housekeeper	1	37.9	46	52.6
101	Housepainter	495—Painters	1	98.5	1	24.9
59	Housewife/Househusband	—	9	4.0	84	29.8
109	Inspector in a manufacturing plant	643—Checkers & inspectors, manufacturing	1	—	—	—
77	Insurance agent	385—Insurance agents	0	47.4	40	36.2
40	Janitor	834—Janitors	0	12.3	67	46.8
26	Keypunch operator	325—Office machine operatives	1	12.7	66	16.1
5	Landscape gardener	964—Gardeners	0	89.7	18	44.9
52	Laundry worker	674—Laundry operative	1	2.8	91	22.5
69	Lawyer	105—Lawyers & judges	9	63.7	30	19.0
16	Locomotive engineer	454—Locomotive engineer	0	4.7	82	75.7
86	Maid (F)/Household dayworker (M)	804—Private hshld. workers, not elsewhere classified	1	0.7	108	47.7
				96.0	9	18.0

Key[a]	Occupational Title[b]	Detailed 1960 Census Category from Which Occupation Drawn[c]	Source Distribution[d]	Percentage Female in Occupation (1970)[e]	Rank Order for Percentage Female[f]	Estimates of Prestige for Occupation[g]
99	Manager of a factory employing 2,000 people	290—Managers, officials, and proprietors, not elsewhere classified, manufacturing	9	4.9	79	63.9
73	Manager of a supermarket	290—Managers, officials, and proprietors, not elsewhere classified, retail dairy	9	17.2	59	47.4
63	Mayor	270—Officials, public administration	0	19.0	58	75.1
15	Metal container maker	775—Operative, metal products	0	12.8	65	29.5
74	Office manager	290—Managers, officials, and proprietors, not elsewhere classified, retail	1	15.5	61	50.3
39	Office secretary	342—Secretaries	1	97.6	4	45.8

43	Owner of a factory employing 2,000 people	290—Managers, officials, and proprietors, not elsewhere classified, manufacturing	9	8.6	71	65.2
82	Parking lot attendant	632—Auto attendants	0	3.5	86	21.6
70	Pastry chef in a restaurant	825—Cooks	0	63.1	31	26.4
102	Person living on welfare	—	9	—	—	—
103	Person who repairs shoes	515—Shoemakers except factory	0	20.3	56	32.8
85	Physician	162—Physicians	9	9.1	69	81.5
80	Piano tuner	504—Piano tuner	1	4.8	81	32.0
98	Plumber	510—Plumbers	0	1.0	107	40.6
53	Police officer	853—Police	0	3.4	88	47.8
22	Post office clerk	340—Postal clerk	0	30.3	49	43.0
78	Powerhouse engineer	520—Stationary engineer	0	1.4	104	35.0
12	Practical nurse	842—Practical nurse	1	96.4	8	41.9
57	Private secretary	342—Secretaries	1	97.6	3	45.8
65	Ragpicker	290—Managers, officials, and proprietors, not elsewhere classified, wholesale	0	5.6	77	44.5

Key[a]	Occupational Title[b]	Detailed 1960 Census Category from Which Occupation Drawn[c]	Source Distribution[d]	Percentage Female in Occupation (1970)[e]	Rank Order for Percentage Female[f]	Estimates of Prestige for Occupation[g]
97	Registered nurse	150—Professional nurses	1	97.3	6	61.5
96	Rubber mixer	775—Operative, rubber & plastic products	1	4.1	83	29.8
8	Salad maker in a hotel	835—Kitchen workers	1	75.9	26	21.8
27	Shirt maker in a manufacturing plant	705—Sewer & stitchers	1	93.6	14	24.9
20	Short-order cook	825—Cooks	1	63.1	32	26.4
33	Social worker	171—Social & welfare workers	1	62.6	33	50.3
56	Sociologist	175—Miscellaneous social scientists	0	35.4	48	65.0
76	Someone who sells shoes in a store	s—Sales, retail	0	38.9	45	28.6
11	Stenographer	345—Stenographer	1	93.6	15	43.3
21	Stockbroker	395—Stock sales	9	9.1	70	50.6
68	Stock clerk	350—Stock clerk	0	22.8	54	23.4

72	Supervisor of telephone operators	353—Telephone operators	1	14.5	63	40.4
93	Telephone operator	353—Telephone operators	1	94.4	12	40.4
89	Textile machine operator	775—Operative, textile machine	1	54.1	36	28.8
25	Tool machinist	465—Machinists	0	3.1	89	47.8
81	Truck driver	715—Truck driver	0	1.4	103	31.3
100	Typesetter	775—Operative, nonelectrical machinery	0	14.9	62	38.0
75	Typist	360—Typists	1	94.1	13	41.3
17	Vegetable grader	775—Operative, food products	0	72.9	27	23.0
60	Waitress/Waiter	875—Waiter	1	89.0	20	20.3
35	Warehouse clerk	370—Clerks, not elsewhere classified	0	22.8	55	36.2
45	Warehouse supervisor	430—Foreman	0	8.0	73	45.3
83	Washing machine repairman	480—Mechanics, not elsewhere classified	0	2.0	97	32.6
54	Welder	721—Welders	0	5.8	76	40.1

Key[a]	Occupational Title[b]	Detailed 1960 Census Category from Which Occupation Drawn[c]	Source Distribution[d]	Percentage Female in Occupation (1970)[e]	Rank Order for Percentage Female[f]	Estimates of Prestige for Occupation[g]
24	Wholesale salesperson	s—Sales, wholesale	0	5.9	75	39.9
32	Yarn washer	775—Operative, textile	1	47.9	39	28.8

[a]Key indicates order of the occupations as kept in computer files and implies nothing about the occupations.

[b]Actual occupational titles used in survey. Note that four of the occupations have alternative versions depending on the sex of the incumbent. These are occupations keyed as nos. 29, 59, 60, and 86. In the treatment with no name, half of the respondents received the male version of the title and half received the female version.

[c]The numbers given represent the detailed occupational census categories of 1960 from which the occupation in the sample was drawn. For convenience, the detailed category title is also provided. 1960 data were derived from U.S. Bureau of the Census (1963).

[d]Indicates which proportional distribution the occupation was drawn from, where:
 1, from distribution of occupations proportional to women in the labor force;
 0, from distribution of occupations proportional to men in the labor force;
 9, occupations added to provide high prestige or non-labor force jobs.

[e]Percentage of women holding jobs in the detailed census category of 1970 most closely approximating the 1960 category from which the occupational stimulus was drawn. Where no good match was available between titles, 1960 figures for percentage women were used. This substitution was made for occupations keyed nos. 31, 50, 61, 86, and 106. 1970 data were derived from U.S. Bureau of the Census (1972, Table 8).

[f]Rank order of occupations according to their percentage of women: 1, occupation with the highest percentage of women; 108, occupation with the lowest percentage of women.

[g]Estimates for the prestige of the occupations were drawn from prior National Opinion Research Center measures of the standing of a particular job title. Whenever it was not possible to fit the exact title, Siegel's (1971) estimates for the detailed categories, based on previously rated jobs within those census categories, are used. All scores are in the standard National Opinion Research Center metric.

APPENDIX C

COMPARISON OF DUNCAN SOCIOECONOMIC INDEX, NATIONAL OPINION RESEARCH CENTER (SIEGEL), AND BOSE NO INCUMBENT SCORES

	Occupation in Sample	Bose No Incumbent Household Scores	NORC/Siegel Scores	Duncan SEI Scores
65	Ragpicker	4.6	45	60
82	Parking lot attendant	8.0	22	33
104	Carhop	8.3	20	33
29	Chambermaid	10.3	14	19
88	Bellhop	10.6	14	27
86	Maid/Dayworker	11.5	18	18
32	Yarn washer	11.8	29	22
40	Janitor	12.5	16	23
8	Salad maker in a hotel	13.8	22	22
52	Laundry worker	14.7	19	28
1	Box packer	15.1	19	31
13	Garbage collector	16.3	13	25
58	Feed grinder	17.8	26	31
96	Rubber mixer	18.1	30	37
50	Babysitter	18.3	23	17
20	Short-order cook	21.5	26	30
60	Waiter/Waitress	22.1	20	33
35	Warehouse clerk	22.4	36	49
64	Boardinghouse keeper	23.7	22	29
46	Coal miner	24.0	25	28
68	Stock clerk	24.4	23	42
18	Flour miller	25.0	25	28
61	Housekeeper	25.3	25	16
2	Fruit harvester for family	26.0	21	17
44	Blacksmith	26.0	36	29
103	Person who repairs shoes	26.0	33	22
27	Shirt maker in a manufacturing plant	26.6	25	26
7	Delivery truck driver	26.9	28	42
17	Vegetable grader	27.4	23	31
19	Electric wire winder	27.6	39	41

APPENDIX C

	Occupation in Sample	Bose No Incumbent Household Scores	NORC/Siegel Scores	Duncan SEI Scores
89	Textile machine operator	27.9	29	22
67	Bookbinder	28.2	31	42
51	Assembly line worker	28.3	27	39
47	Floor finisher	28.8	30	32
4	Fireman in boiler room	29.2	33	31
94	Hospital aide	29.5	36	33
15	Metal container maker	31.1	30	34
48	Cotton farmer	32.4	41	20
110	Cattledriver for family	33.0	21	17
92	Dress cutter	33.3	26	29
34	File clerk	34.0	30	45
66	Cashier	35.6	31	44
76	Sells shoes in a store	35.9	29	46
84	Automobile refinisher	36.9	29	32
49	Butcher in a shop	38.8	32	40
83	Washing machine repairman	38.8	33	38
70	Pastry chef in a restaurant	39.4	26	30
108	Hairdresser	39.4	33	46
101	House painter	39.7	30	32
81	Truck driver	40.1	31	31
5	Landscape gardener	40.5	23	23
80	Piano tuner	41.0	32	43
6	Beautician	42.1	33	46
22	Post office clerk	42.3	43	51
100	Typesetter	42.6	38	38
26	Keypunch operator	44.6	45	50
75	Typist	44.9	41	47
107	Auto mechanic	44.9	37	35
24	Wholesale salesperson	46.2	40	55
93	Telephone operator	46.2	40	51
54	Welder	46.8	40	37

	Occupation in Sample	Bose No Incumbent Household Scores	NORC/Siegel Scores	Duncan SEI Scores
25	Tool machinist	48.4	48	44
10	Florist	49.7	50	51
28	Bookkeeper	50.0	48	50
39	Office secretary	51.3	46	54
109	Inspector in a manufacturing plant	51.3	36	47
11	Stenographer	52.6	43	52
16	Locomotive engineer	52.9	48	47
23	Carpenter	53.5	43	34
3	Assembly line supervisor, manufacturing	53.8	45	54
45	Warehouse supervisor	54.2	45	54
36	Dental assistant	54.8	48	45
12	Practical nurse	56.4	42	37
62	Car dealer	57.1	44	53
73	Manager of a supermarket	57.1	47	51
53	Police officer	58.3	48	50
98	Plumber	58.7	41	42
72	Supervisor of telephone operators	60.3	40	51
87	Floor supervisor in hospital	60.3	62	50
57	Private secretary	60.9	46	54
71	Electrician	62.5	49	51
77	Insurance agent	62.5	47	57
105	Artist	62.8	57	62
91	Hospital lab technician	63.1	61	50
33	Social worker	63.2	50	72
14	Circulation director of newspaper	63.5	61	69
38	Hotel manager	64.1	53	51
78	Powerhouse engineer	64.5	35	54
106	Grade school teacher	65.4	60	74
37	Administrative assistant	67.8	36	53
74	Office manager	68.3	50	52

APPENDIX C

	Occupation in Sample	Bose No Incumbent Household Scores	NORC/Siegel Scores	Duncan SEI Scores
99	Manager, factory of 2,000 employees	69.2	64	69
31	High school teacher	70.2	63	78
95	Accountant	71.2	57	70
56	Sociologist	74.7	65	83
97	Registered nurse	75.0	62	50
30	Chiropractor	75.3	60	74
41	Building construction contractor	78.9	55	57
9	Electrical engineer	79.5	69	83
55	Advertising executive	80.8	60	75
21	Stockbroker	81.7	51	70
43	Owner of factory employing 2,000	81.7	65	61
42	City superintendent of schools	87.8	67	78
90	Architect	88.8	71	87
69	Lawyer	90.1	76	97
79	College professor	90.1	78	84
63	Mayor	92.2	75	53
85	Physician	95.8	82	112
Mean score ($\bar{X}$)		45	40	45

Occupations are presented in the ascending rank order of the Bose no incumbent household sample scores. The 108 labor force jobs are from the Bose study described herein.

Sources: (a) Bose No Incumbent Household Scores were developed as described in Chapter 2 of this volume. Appendix D provides these scores for the incumbent treatments, as well as all of the ratings given by the college sample. (b) NORC/Siegel scores are created in the same manner as described in Appendix B, footnote g. Estimates for the prestige of particular job titles were drawn from prior National Opinion Research Center measures of prestige. Whenever it was not possible to fit the exact title, Siegel's (1971) estimates for the 1960 detailed census categories, based on an average of previously rated jobs in those categories, were used. All scores are in the standard NORC metric. (c) Duncan socioeconomic scores were developed using the relational formula: No Incumbent Prestige = 0.0039(Median Dollars Income of Men) + 5.0(Median Years Education of Men) - 32.8. See Chapter 5 for further details.

APPENDIX D

PRESTIGE SCORES
FOR THE ORIGINAL 110 JOBS,
BY TREATMENT AND SAMPLE

Key	Occupation[a]	No Incumbent		Mixed Incumbents						All Female Incumbents		All Male Incumbents	
				Female Names		Male Names							
		College	Household	College	Household	College	Household			College	Household	College	Household
95	Accountant	74.3	71.2	69.9	69.9	69.2	74.4			73.5	74.7	69.9	68.8
37	Administrative assistant	73.2	67.8	70.9	67.0	72.2	67.9			72.9	69.9	68.6	68.1
55	Advertising executive	82.1	80.8	81.9	80.4	81.0	75.6			84.1	79.8	85.3	76.6
90	Architect	85.7	88.8	86.6	82.7	85.0	88.1			86.9	85.5	85.3	84.5
105	Artist	62.9	62.8	68.9	62.8	63.9	58.6			66.2	66.1	59.0	56.9
3	Assembly line supervisor in a manufacturing plant	55.7	53.8	51.8	57.5	49.4	51.6			50.0	54.8	55.4	50.0
51	Assembly line worker	30.7	28.3	21.5	26.6	22.9	36.9			24.1	35.6	25.3	27.6
107	Auto mechanic	41.1	44.9	39.3	49.4	40.8	45.2			37.5	48.1	39.7	41.3
84	Automobile refinisher	35.4	36.9	30.6	38.8	34.8	27.5			29.6	36.5	31.7	39.4
50	Babysitter	19.6	18.3	17.9	18.3	20.9	17.8			22.6	25.0	16.0	15.4
6	Beautician	42.1	42.1	40.9	47.4	38.1	44.2			37.2	46.3	37.2	42.3
88	Bellhop	18.6	10.6	11.9	17.3	14.0	9.4			16.2	20.2	13.5	14.7
44	Blacksmith	36.8	26.0	28.4	26.6	31.3	30.3			32.3	37.2	32.1	34.6
64	Boardinghouse keeper	35.4	23.7	30.8	28.2	30.2	26.9			30.5	36.5	35.3	29.4
67	Bookbinder	32.1	28.2	24.7	32.4	33.2	33.8			30.5	35.9	32.4	33.0
28	Bookkeeper	56.4	50.0	53.3	53.4	48.7	55.1			50.0	61.8	53.5	55.6
1	Box packer	13.9	15.1	17.6	16.6	11.2	16.0			12.8	23.1	17.9	13.8
41	Building construction contractor	74.3	78.9	68.9	79.4	67.9	77.3			68.9	78.2	68.9	74.4
49	Butcher in a shop	35.0	38.8	35.9	30.4	29.9	44.7			34.8	48.1	37.8	38.5
62	Car dealer	56.1	57.1	52.2	53.8	52.1	57.5			51.5	60.3	53.2	50.6
104	Carhop	13.6	8.3	13.1	15.2	12.2	9.9			15.5	21.4	15.4	13.5

Key	Occupation[a]	No Incumbent		Mixed Incumbents						All Female Incumbents		All Male Incumbents	
				Female Names		Male Names							
		College	Household	College	Household	College	Household			College	Household	College	Household
23	Carpenter	56.4	53.5	49.7	47.2	44.1	53.2			48.5	54.5	50.3	51.9
66	Cashier	36.1	35.6	29.5	42.3	34.5	43.3			31.7	41.7	30.1	35.6
110	Cattledriver working for own family	34.6	33.0	29.8	32.5	28.6	35.9			36.6	40.7	37.5	32.4
30	Chiropractor	77.5	75.3	77.1	76.6	72.7	76.6			80.8	70.1	70.2	75.3
14	Circulation director of a newspaper	62.1	63.5	57.6	60.9	64.4	56.6			61.6	66.2	59.0	52.6
42	City superintendent of schools	85.0	87.8	88.1	85.0	86.5	82.4			90.9	90.4	82.1	85.6
46	Coal miner	23.2	24.0	19.7	26.6	21.9	26.6			19.8	32.1	23.1	24.1
79	College professor	85.0	90.1	86.2	87.5	83.0	87.5			86.3	90.1	81.4	85.3
48	Cotton farmer	28.6	32.4	31.1	30.1	31.1	29.7			25.0	41.3	35.6	26.6
7	Delivery truck driver	29.3	26.9	27.7	31.6	23.4	31.7			22.9	38.1	24.7	28.1
36	Dental assistant	61.4	54.8	60.3	60.3	56.6	57.7			56.4	56.7	53.8	54.4
92	Dress cutter	36.1	33.3	28.4	34.0	30.6	31.9			29.3	40.4	29.8	31.9
9	Electrical engineer	77.1	79.5	72.9	78.8	79.2	79.8			79.6	78.2	75.3	78.1
71	Electrician	60.4	62.5	56.7	64.7	61.9	57.2			55.8	60.3	55.8	58.4
19	Electric wire winder	31.8	27.6	28.7	34.9	24.4	37.8			26.2	37.2	26.9	36.9
58	Feed grinder	22.5	17.8	16.7	20.4	17.1	17.3			17.7	27.7	22.8	23.3
34	File clerk	40.7	34.0	37.5	42.5	36.3	39.7			35.4	40.1	36.9	40.6
4	Fireman in a boiler room	28.2	29.2	26.5	32.2	24.4	37.8			26.5	41.7	29.2	32.1
47	Floor finisher	28.6	28.8	21.9	30.8	24.7	38.5			26.5	35.6	27.9	28.8
87	Floor supervisor in a hospital	63.2	60.3	60.5	64.5	63.7	54.1			59.1	58.3	60.9	54.5

	Occupation										
10	Florist	46.8	49.7	47.3	50.0	47.1	46.5	45.7	51.6	46.2	46.3
18	Flour miller	28.2	25.0	29.0	23.3	24.0	27.9	18.3	29.9	27.2	23.1
2	Fruit harvester, working for own family	29.6	26.0	27.4	25.0	23.0	28.8	29.6	39.7	34.0	25.6
13	Garbage collector	12.5	16.3	10.1	15.9	11.9	20.5	17.4	18.6	12.8	15.4
106	Grade school teacher	64.6	65.4	61.3	68.4	65.4	64.5	64.9	66.7	59.3	59.4
108	Hairdresser	42.5	39.4	38.4	44.4	39.8	38.8	33.8	41.3	37.2	41.6
31	High school teacher	67.5	70.2	66.1	64.4	64.5	71.5	67.7	76.6	62.8	67.8
94	Hospital aide	39.3	29.5	37.5	33.3	39.9	30.0	37.8	34.9	34.3	30.9
91	Hospital lab technician	68.9	63.1	61.6	63.8	69.7	66.7	64.3	63.5	59.3	65.4
29	Hotel chambermaid (F)/ Hotel bedmaker (M)	20.4	10.3	17.9	13.8	10.9	12.5	15.9	19.9	17.6	11.6
38	Hotel manager	61.4	64.1	63.1	69.1	60.9	68.9	66.5	63.5	60.9	62.5
61	Housekeeper	28.6	25.3	18.3	29.5	26.8	23.1	27.7	34.3	24.7	28.4
101	House painter	40.7	39.7	33.1	44.7	36.3	29.8	32.9	42.0	36.5	30.3
59	Housewife/Househusband—										
	wife	46.1	51.0	36.2	43.6	—	—	46.0	53.3	—	—
	husband	31.5	14.5	—	—	27.4	23.8	—	—	28.5	18.1
109	Inspector in a manufacturing plant	59.3	51.3	54.2	51.3	51.3	47.8	51.2	55.4	54.2	51.3
77	Insurance agent	63.6	62.5	58.9	60.6	59.5	62.2	63.4	60.6	59.9	57.2
40	Janitor	15.7	12.5	11.3	10.0	9.6	15.1	13.1	15.4	9.9	7.2
26	Keypunch operator	48.9	44.6	45.2	45.1	45.4	52.3	40.5	48.4	45.2	44.9
5	Landscape gardener	42.1	40.5	46.3	34.5	40.6	39.4	39.3	49.3	44.2	41.3
52	Laundry worker	18.2	14.7	13.2	17.6	14.9	15.9	15.2	21.8	15.4	13.7
69	Lawyer	93.9	90.1	93.6	91.7	92.1	90.6	96.6	87.8	93.3	92.2

Key	Occupation[a]	No Incumbent		Mixed Incumbents				All Female Incumbents		All Male Incumbents	
				Female Names		Male Names					
		College	Household	College	Household	College	Household	College	Household	College	Household
16	Locomotive engineer	51.1	52.9	49.7	54.7	45.8	59.6	48.5	56.4	46.8	54.7
86	Maid (F)/Household day-worker (M)	22.5	11.5	13.8	16.6	20.5	15.9	14.9	19.9	17.3	13.8
99	Manager of a factory employing 2,000 people	69.3	69.2	72.5	71.9	70.3	72.8	69.8	67.9	75.6	79.4
73	Manager of a supermarket	56.8	57.1	59.3	61.5	58.2	55.9	59.1	59.3	58.3	58.4
63	Mayor	88.9	92.2	92.9	92.1	92.1	90.3	91.8	92.3	92.9	96.3
15	Metal container maker	31.8	31.1	25.9	32.2	22.8	32.4	24.7	32.1	23.7	29.4
74	Office manager	67.1	68.3	62.8	70.8	62.8	66.3	67.7	67.3	60.3	64.7
39	Office secretary	53.9	51.3	46.6	62.2	46.8	57.4	47.6	60.3	45.8	57.5
43	Owner of a factory employing 2,000 people	80.4	81.7	79.6	82.5	82.4	86.9	81.1	75.6	76.6	85.9
82	Parking lot attendant	14.6	8.0	12.5	13.8	12.5	10.9	14.9	18.9	15.1	10.9
70	Pastry chef in a restaurant	42.9	39.4	35.6	36.9	37.5	28.1	34.1	41.1	35.3	37.5
102	Person living on welfare	3.9	8.2	2.5	5.3	5.0	1.9	4.6	13.2	5.1	8.1
103	Person who repairs shoes	31.1	26.0	26.2	30.9	29.5	26.3	25.3	38.1	26.9	26.9
85	Physician	94.3	95.8	95.4	90.1	93.8	95.9	96.6	89.7	92.3	93.6
80	Piano tuner	46.4	41.0	38.8	43.9	40.8	31.3	36.3	46.1	40.4	34.9
98	Plumber	54.3	58.7	42.9	56.4	47.0	52.5	43.6	57.7	49.0	51.9
53	Police officer	56.8	58.3	55.9	52.9	56.8	55.0	59.1	57.7	49.4	58.1
22	Post office clerk	46.4	42.3	41.4	42.8	39.1	48.1	38.1	45.5	40.4	41.9
78	Powerhouse engineer	57.5	64.5	59.5	66.1	61.3	63.5	57.9	59.5	62.5	68.6

12	Practical nurse	59.6	56.4	62.2	58.4	58.3	61.5	58.5	59.0	54.5	58.1
57	Private secretary	61.1	60.9	52.0	66.0	61.0	69.1	59.1	59.3	58.7	61.6
65	Ragpicker	6.4	4.6	2.6	5.8	4.6	5.9	5.5	14.1	5.4	4.4
97	Registered nurse	71.1	75.0	68.6	71.2	72.6	72.8	71.3	69.2	62.2	68.8
96	Rubber mixer	21.4	18.1	16.7	22.4	24.7	28.8	19.2	29.6	21.8	23.0
8	Salad maker in a hotel	22.1	13.8	21.3	19.9	17.0	20.1	16.2	26.3	20.8	20.2
27	Shirt maker in a manufacturing plant	30.7	26.6	23.8	25.9	23.0	34.0	22.0	32.1	23.4	31.6
20	Short-order cook	23.9	21.5	21.1	17.7	19.4	26.0	21.6	24.0	22.1	18.1
33	Social worker	62.5	63.2	64.6	56.6	62.2	60.6	62.5	62.8	58.0	53.1
56	Sociologist	73.6	74.7	76.6	71.2	75.0	72.7	78.0	68.8	70.2	67.0
76	Someone who sells shoes in a store	35.4	35.9	35.9	33.0	31.5	31.3	32.0	34.3	31.1	33.1
11	Stenographer	55.0	52.6	50.0	56.3	44.2	56.4	51.5	55.6	47.4	55.3
21	Stockbroker	77.9	81.7	79.5	80.9	80.6	80.8	81.7	77.7	80.8	79.9
68	Stock clerk	31.8	24.4	34.0	32.7	36.9	28.1	30.5	30.3	30.8	31.3
72	Supervisor of telephone operators	57.1	60.3	57.4	61.9	56.1	61.3	56.4	58.7	56.7	59.0
93	Telephone operator	41.4	46.2	36.6	48.1	39.4	49.1	38.7	45.2	39.7	46.9
89	Textile machine operator	36.8	27.9	25.3	31.7	32.8	31.6	30.5	40.2	32.7	33.1
25	Tool machinist	42.5	48.4	43.5	44.1	35.5	52.6	34.1	49.0	38.1	45.3
81	Truck driver	36.1	40.1	25.3	38.5	30.7	37.2	25.6	44.2	34.4	35.6
100	Typesetter	40.0	42.6	36.6	47.2	37.8	46.5	38.1	49.7	38.8	47.1
75	Typist	46.4	44.9	40.8	48.7	43.8	46.6	41.5	48.7	41.3	46.6
17	Vegetable grader	22.1	27.4	22.6	16.1	20.2	25.6	18.6	28.9	25.6	20.7
60	Waitress/Waiter	27.5	22.1	20.2	24.4	25.0	27.2	23.2	28.2	23.7	22.1

| | | No Incumbent | | Mixed Incumbents | | | | All Female Incumbents | | All Male Incumbents | |
| | | | | Female Names | | Male Names | | | | | |
Key	Occupation[a]	College	Household	College	Household	College	Household	College	Household	College	Household
35	Warehouse clerk	31.4	22.4	30.3	28.7	31.9	31.7	32.9	35.9	33.3	34.3
45	Warehouse supervisor	51.8	54.2	53.1	48.4	50.9	55.6	53.4	55.1	55.1	50.0
83	Washing machine repairman	35.4	38.8	30.6	41.7	33.9	30.3	33.2	45.8	32.4	36.3
54	Welder	43.2	46.8	38.3	42.9	40.8	49.1	38.7	45.5	38.1	43.1
24	Wholesale salesperson	42.5	46.2	42.0	42.9	42.4	42.0	42.4	47.7	42.0	40.7
32	Yarn washer	15.4	11.8	16.7	14.7	12.2	13.5	13.4	26.0	17.9	11.1
Mean score ($\bar{X}$)—female respondents		45.7	43.1	43.0	46.1	42.7	45.9	43.6	49.2	44.7	46.7
Mean score ($\bar{X}$)—male respondents		47.1	46.8	43.9	46.0	44.8	46.4	44.1	48.7	42.5	42.6

[a] Arranged alphabetically.

APPENDIX E

BOSE INDEX FOR CENSUS OCCUPATIONS: 1960, 1970, AND 1980 CENSUSES

1960 BOSE INDEX[a]

Three-Digit Occupation Code	Three-Digit Industry Code	Class of Worker	Income Median ($)	Education Median (years)	Bose Index
000	b	b	4532	12.8	58
010	b	b	5500	13.1	65
012	b	b	5976	13.8	71
013	b	b	5658	16.6	85
014	b	b	4351	15.1	70
015	b	b	4256	12.4	55
020	b	b	3720	16.0	72
021	b	b	5596	16.5	84
022	b	b	3378	15.2	66
023	b	b	2219	12.8	47
030	b	b	6988	17.4	96
031	b	b	NA	10.5	NA
032	b	b	5488	17.3	88
034	b	b	4750	17.4	85
035	b	b	7000	17.5	96
040	b	b	5524	17.1	87
041	b	b	976	17.5	67
042	b	b	5268	17.4	87
043	b	b	6199	17.3	91
045	b	b	8049	17.3	100
050	b	b	5715	17.4	89
051	b	b	9000	17.5	100
052	b	b	NA	17.5	NA
053	b	b	5907	17.4	90
054	b	b	5337	17.4	88
060	b	b	5935	17.3	90
070	b	b	3126	12.5	50
071	b	b	3975	16.0	73
072	b	b	4782	13.0	61
073	b	b	3670	13.2	56
074	b	b	4685	12.9	60
075	b	b	4233	14.6	67
080	b	b	7728	15.2	87
081	b	b	5268	12.6	61
082	b	b	6861	16.2	88
083	b	b	5585	15.2	77
084	b	b	5916	12.8	65
085	b	b	6000	14.9	77
090	b	b	7425	14.5	82
091	b	b	3500	12.5	52

APPENDIX E

Three-Digit Occupation Code	Three-Digit Industry Code	Class of Worker	Income Median ($)	Education Median (years)	Bose Index
092	b	b	11187	16.0	100
093	b	b	6496	13.8	73
101	b	b	3668	12.4	52
102	b	b	5265	16.5	82
103	b	b	2279	10.7	36
104	b	b	5135	12.7	61
105	b	b	5681	17.0	87
111	b	b	4146	16.2	75
120	b	b	1503	14.8	55
130	b	b	3525	12.6	52
131	b	b	4958	16.7	82
134	b	b	7500	17.0	96
135	b	b	6381	16.4	87
140	b	b	7000	16.6	91
145	b	b	4820	13.7	65
150	b	b	3830	13.2	57
151	b	b	893	13.0	42
152	b	b	3260	15.0	64
153	b	b	4656	16.5	79
154	b	b	4877	13.1	62
160	b	b	4897	16.2	79
161	b	b	3272	12.4	50
162	b	b	6562	17.4	93
163	b	b	4680	15.4	73
164	b	b	3715	12.3	52
165	b	b	4145	14.7	67
170	b	b	2376	13.4	51
171	b	b	4654	16.5	79
172	b	b	5180	15.9	79
173	b	b	6020	17.4	91
174	b	b	4650	13.0	60
175	b	b	4318	16.3	77
180	b	b	4977	16.5	81
181	b	b	4738	12.7	59
182	b	2,6,NA	4781	16.4	79
182	b	1,3,4,5	1795	16.1	63
183	b	2,6,NA	5122	16.8	83
183	b	1,3,4,5	3169	17.0	75
184	b	b	3834	16.1	73
185	b	b	3670	13.2	56
190	b	b	4288	12.3	54
191	b	b	4179	12.6	55

Three-Digit Occupation Code	Three-Digit Industry Code	Class of Worker	Income Median ($)	Education Median (years)	Bose Index
192	b	b	4044	12.7	55
193	b	b	4344	16.1	76
194	b	b	6025	17.1	89
195	b	b	4820	16.1	78
200	b	b	921	8.8	19
222	b	b	1583	12.2	41
250	b	b	3941	12.4	53
251	b	b	3475	12.2	50
252	b	b	7500	9.8	56
253	b	b	3743	12.5	53
254	b	b	2921	11.5	43
260	906–916	b	4961	12.2	57
260	926	b	3740	12.6	53
260	936	b	3410	12.4	51
260	Not 906–936	b	4510	12.4	56
262	b	b	1511	11.1	34
265	b	b	6475	10.5	55
270	906–916	b	5704	12.8	64
270	926	b	4833	13.0	61
270	936	b	3705	12.6	53
270	Not 906–936	b	4272	12.7	56
275	b	b	4457	12.5	56
280	b	b	4035	12.3	53
285	b	b	4704	12.6	58
290	016–156	4,5	3131	12.1	48
290	016–156	Not 4,5	4330	12.7	57
290	196	4,5	6109	12.3	63
290	196	Not 4,5	4907	12.6	59
290	206–459	4,5	4829	12.3	57
290	206–459	Not 4,5	5002	12.6	59
290	506–526	4,5	3891	12.3	52
290	506–526	Not 4,5	4598	12.7	58
290	536–579	4,5	5763	12.8	64
290	536–579	Not 4,5	4826	12.6	59
290	606–629	4,5	4735	12.4	57
290	606–629	Not 4,5	4756	12.6	58
290	636–637	4,5	1928	9.9	30
290	636–637	Not 4,5	3185	11.3	43
290	638–639	4,5	2091	12.1	43
290	638–639	Not 4,5	3630	12.3	51
290	646–647	4,5	3296	12.4	50
290	646–647	Not 4,5	3700	12.3	52

APPENDIX E 155

Three-Digit Occupation Code	Three-Digit Industry Code	Class of Worker	Income Median ($)	Education Median (years)	Bose Index
290	648-649	4,5	4185	12.4	54
290	648-649	Not 4,5	4346	12.7	57
290	656	4,5	3476	12.4	51
290	656	Not 4,5	4983	12.6	59
290	657	4,5	1692	10.0	29
290	657	Not 4,5	4375	12.4	55
290	658	4,5	2680	12.7	46
290	658	Not 4,5	3471	12.2	50
290	659	4,5	2474	10.4	36
290	659	Not 4,5	3126	11.1	42
290	666-676	4,5	3298	12.2	49
290	666-676	Not 4,5	4118	12.5	55
290	678-696	4,5	2680	12.2	46
290	678-696	Not 4,5	3471	12.2	50
290	706-716	4,5	4975	12.8	60
290	706-716	Not 4,5	4354	12.6	56
290	726-736	4,5	3792	12.6	54
290	726-736	Not 4,5	4357	12.6	56
290	806-807	4,5	4573	12.9	59
290	806-807	Not 4,5	4644	12.8	59
290	808	4,5	3778	11.0	45
290	808	Not 4,5	4746	12.5	58
290	809	4,5	3925	12.3	53
290	809	Not 4,5	3898	12.4	53
290	816-839	4,5	2434	11.7	42
290	816-839	Not 4,5	2817	11.9	45
290	846-998	4,5	3131	12.1	48
290	846-998	Not 4,5	4330	12.7	57
290	999, NA	4,5	2722	11.8	44
290	999, NA	Not 4,5	4221	12.5	55
301	b	b	4156	12.7	56
302	b	b	2860	13.1	52
303	b	b	2825	12.5	48
304	b	b	4000	12.7	55
305	b	b	3379	12.5	51
310	b	b	3414	12.5	51
312	b	b	2835	12.0	46
313	b	b	3136	12.3	49
314	b	b	3039	12.0	47
315	b	b	3263	12.5	51
320	b	b	3185	12.2	48
321	b	b	3849	12.6	54

Three-Digit Occupation Code	Three-Digit Industry Code	Class of Worker	Income Median ($)	Education Median (years)	Bose Index
323	b	b	3569	12.2	50
324	b	b	2336	11.8	42
325	b	b	3674	12.4	52
333	b	b	3909	12.4	53
340	b	b	4099	12.4	54
341	b	b	3077	12.5	50
342	b	b	3812	12.6	54
343	b	b	3136	11.5	44
345	b	b	3742	12.6	53
350	b	b	3357	12.0	48
351	b	b	2620	10.5	36
352	b	b	4618	12.3	56
353	b	b	3599	12.2	50
354	b	b	4405	12.7	57
360	b	b	3420	12.5	51
370	016-196	b	2838	12.2	47
370	206-459	b	3677	12.3	51
370	506-579	b	3920	12.4	53
370	606-696	b	2979	12.3	48
370	706-736	b	3395	12.4	51
370	806-849	b	2838	12.2	47
370	867-898	b	3069	12.6	50
370	906-936	b	4064	12.6	55
370	998	b	2838	12.2	47
370	999, NA	b	3517	12.4	51
380	b	b	4330	12.8	57
381	b	b	1500	12.3	41
382	b	b	2450	12.1	44
383	b	b	921	12.1	37
385	b	b	3659	12.6	53
390	b	b	773	10.0	25
393	b	b	3812	12.6	54
394	016-196	b	2569	12.0	44
394	206-459	b	2606	11.5	42
394	506-579	b	2569	12.0	44
394	606-608	b	3459	12.2	50
394	609	b	2562	11.8	43
394	616-629	b	3459	12.2	50
394	636-637	b	2020	10.7	35
394	638	b	2423	11.7	42
394	639	b	1860	11.0	35
394	646-647	b	2444	11.8	43

APPENDIX E

Three-Digit Occupation Code	Three-Digit Industry Code	Class of Worker	Income Median ($)	Education Median (years)	Bose Index
394	648-649	b	2337	12.0	43
394	656	b	2961	12.2	47
394	657-696	b	2337	12.0	43
394	706-998	b	2569	12.0	44
394	999, NA	b	2331	11.5	40
395	b	b	4386	12.8	58
401	b	b	2441	9.7	31
402	b	b	2988	12.1	47
403	b	b	NA	10.5	NA
404	b	b	3299	9.9	36
405	b	b	3667	9.5	36
410	b	b	3015	11.2	42
411	b	b	3415	10.0	37
413	b	b	1475	12.0	39
414	b	b	3520	12.2	50
415	b	b	4753	10.7	48
420	b	b	2942	12.4	48
421	b	b	4712	11.6	52
423	b	b	NA	12.5	NA
424	b	b	3673	11.0	44
425	b	b	4119	10.7	45
430	016-156	b	3593	11.8	48
430	196	b	5488	10.9	52
430	206-236	b	3805	10.9	44
430	237-249	b	4792	12.0	55
430	256-258	b	4890	12.1	56
430	259	b	4262	11.3	49
430	267	b	6488	10.5	55
430	268-276	b	5413	12.5	61
430	286-296	b	3805	10.9	44
430	306-329	b	3916	10.5	43
430	346-367	b	3377	10.1	38
430	386-459	b	3916	10.5	43
430	506	b	5250	8.5	38
430	507-526	b	4630	12.5	57
430	536-579	b	5639	12.3	61
430	606-998	b	3593	11.8	48
430	999, NA	b	3781	10.9	44
431	b	b	3238	9.5	34
432	b	b	2171	9.4	28
434	b	b	4013	9.8	39
435	b	b	3748	8.4	30

Three-Digit Occupation Code	Three-Digit Industry Code	Class of Worker	Income Median ($)	Education Median (years)	Bose Index
444	b	b	3071	10.8	40
450	016-156	b	3168	9.5	33
450	196	b	3172	12.7	51
450	206-459	b	3168	9.5	33
450	506	b	4833	8.8	38
450	507-579	b	4505	10.2	44
450	606-998	b	3168	9.5	33
450	999, NA	b	3285	9.6	35
451	b	b	2668	10.5	37
452	b	b	3500	11.7	47
453	b	b	4204	12.1	53
454	b	b	6500	12.3	65
460	b	b	5475	12.7	62
461	b	b	3500	8.5	29
465	b	b	3593	10.1	39
470	b	b	3756	12.0	50
471	b	b	5238	11.6	55
472	b	b	3968	10.6	43
473	b	b	3500	12.7	53
474	b	b	3726	11.9	49
475	b	b	1975	12.0	42
480	016-156	b	2374	9.3	29
480	196	b	3405	9.0	32
480	206-459	b	3667	10.2	40
480	506-579	b	3640	11.1	45
480	606-696	b	2717	11.5	42
480	706-736	b	2374	9.3	29
480	806-809	b	3005	10.9	40
480	816-898	b	2374	9.3	29
480	906-936	b	4475	11.2	49
480	998	b	2374	8.3	29
480	999, NA	b	3416	10.3	39
490	b	b	1977	12.0	42
491	b	b	7048	7.9	43
492	b	b	3656	10.3	40
493	b	b	2342	12.1	44
494	b	b	3442	11.4	45
495	b	b	2916	11.7	44
501	b	b	1976	8.8	24
502	b	b	4500	12.2	55
503	b	b	3827	12.0	50
504	b	b	3373	11.5	46

APPENDIX E

Three-Digit Occupation Code	Three-Digit Industry Code	Class of Worker	Income Median ($)	Education Median (years)	Bose Index
505	b	b	3333	8.5	29
510	b	b	4314	10.5	44
512	b	b	3795	11.1	45
513	b	b	3700	9.8	38
514	b	b	8000	10.5	62
515	b	b	1704	9.5	26
520	b	b	4418	12.5	56
521	b	b	3500	10.5	41
523	b	b	3863	11.5	48
524	b	b	2770	8.9	28
525	b	b	4519	11.0	48
530	b	b	4666	11.4	51
535	b	b	3097	9.4	33
545	b	b	3342	10.5	40
555	b	b	1860	12.3	43
601	b	b	501	12.0	34
602	b	b	NA	12.5	NA
603	b	b	NA	NA	NA
604	b	b	4975	12.5	59
605	b	b	3744	12.3	52
610	b	b	5000	12.6	59
612	b	b	NA	NA	NA
613	b	b	4024	8.5	32
614	b	b	NA	13.0	NA
615	b	b	2732	11.5	42
620	b	b	1756	11.2	36
621	b	b	2024	11.3	38
630	b	b	4008	11.4	48
631	b	b	3627	10.4	41
632	b	b	2145	10.5	34
634	b	b	3500	10.6	41
635	b	b	NA	11.3	NA
640	b	b	5000	11.3	52
641	b	b	2806	11.7	44
642	b	b	4373	12.0	53
643	b	b	3433	10.2	39
645	b	b	2000	12.0	42
650	b	b	2000	11.1	37
651	b	b	2107	9.5	28
652	b	b	2588	10.4	36
653	b	b	4109	10.1	41
654	b	b	2172	8.6	24

Three-Digit Occupation Code	Three-Digit Industry Code	Class of Worker	Income Median ($)	Education Median (years)	Bose Index
670	b	b	4000	9.9	40
671	b	b	2998	9.1	30
672	b	b	2500	10.0	33
673	b	b	2628	9.2	29
674	b	b	2016	8.9	25
675	b	b	2741	10.0	34
680	b	b	2433	9.8	32
685	126	b	3475	10.0	38
685	136	b	5526	8.1	37
685	146	b	3490	12.1	49
685	156	b	3475	10.0	38
685	Not 126-156	b	3734	9.7	37
690	b	b	NA	10.5	NA
691	b	b	3500	10.5	41
692	b	b	3750	10.2	40
693	b	b	3119	9.7	34
694	b	b	3273	9.9	36
695	b	b	3234	11.9	47
701	b	b	2793	8.9	28
703	b	b	3452	8.7	30
704	b	b	3173	9.1	31
705	b	b	2633	8.9	28
710	b	b	2757	7.7	21
712	b	b	3213	8.7	29
713	b	b	4988	10.9	50
714	b	b	2850	11.1	41
715	b	b	3635	10.4	41
720	b	b	3331	8.6	29
721	b	b	3690	10.5	41
775	016-156	b	2479	10.2	34
775	196	b	2935	10.1	36
775	206	b	2479	10.2	34
775	207	b	2793	9.5	32
775	208	b	2506	8.9	27
775	209	b	2951	8.9	29
775	216	b	3528	10.0	38
775	217	b	3744	8.9	33
775	218	b	3252	10.3	38
775	219	b	3207	9.6	34
775	236	b	3512	9.9	37
775	237	b	4356	9.9	41
775	238	b	4027	10.1	41

APPENDIX E

Three-Digit Occupation Code	Three-Digit Industry Code	Class of Worker	Income Median ($)	Education Median (years)	Bose Index
775	239	b	3932	9.8	39
775	246	b	3582	9.3	34
775	247	b	3056	9.9	35
775	248	b	3741	9.6	37
775	249	b	3701	9.5	36
775	256	b	3553	8.9	32
775	257	b	4095	10.3	42
775	258	b	3827	9.7	38
775	259	b	3632	10.5	41
775	267	b	4424	10.0	42
775	268	b	4446	10.8	47
775	269	b	3492	9.0	32
775	276	b	4196	10.7	45
775	286	b	3613	9.9	38
775	287	b	3984	10.6	43
775	289	b	3371	10.1	38
775	296	b	2759	9.1	29
775	306	b	2838	9.0	29
775	307	b	3000	10.1	36
775	308	b	2490	8.6	25
775	309	b	3506	10.2	39
775	316	b	3238	9.5	34
775	317	b	2897	9.0	29
775	318	b	3837	9.2	35
775	319	b	3000	9.0	30
775	326	b	2792	8.8	28
775	329	b	2988	8.6	28
775	346	b	2651	9.3	30
775	347	b	2886	9.4	32
775	348	b	3076	8.7	29
775	349	b	2767	8.6	27
775	356	b	2727	8.9	28
775	359	b	2592	8.9	27
775	367	b	2572	8.8	27
775	386	b	3676	10.2	40
775	387	b	3155	9.2	32
775	389	b	3296	9.5	34
775	396	b	2363	12.0	43
775	398	b	3228	10.2	38
775	406	b	4184	10.4	43
775	407	b	3721	10.2	40
775	408	b	3422	8.9	31

Three-Digit Occupation Code	Three-Digit Industry Code	Class of Worker	Income Median ($)	Education Median (years)	Bose Index
775	409	b	3507	9.8	37
775	416	b	4318	12.1	53
775	419	b	2990	10.7	39
775	426	b	3834	9.8	38
775	429	b	3144	9.8	35
775	436	b	3276	8.5	28
775	437	b	2647	9.0	28
775	438	b	2651	8.9	28
775	459	b	2660	9.5	31
775	506	b	4279	12.2	54
775	507-526	b	3635	9.8	37
775	536-579	b	3648	12.2	51
775	606-696	b	2642	9.3	30
775	706-736	b	2479	10.2	34
775	806-809	b	3005	10.4	38
775	816-839	b	2242	8.8	25
775	846-898	b	2479	10.2	34
775	906-936	b	4034	10.7	44
775	998	b	2479	10.2	34
775	999, NA	b	3011	9.3	32
801	b	b	666	9.6	22
802	b	b	1201	8.6	19
803	b	b	603	7.7	11
804	b	b	940	8.4	17
810	b	b	2407	10.8	37
812	b	b	1735	11.2	36
813	b	b	2070	11.1	37
814	b	b	2236	11.3	39
815	b	b	2532	10.4	35
820	b	b	2500	9.3	29
821	b	b	1305	10.0	27
823	b	b	1684	8.7	22
824	b	b	1721	8.5	21
825	b	b	1959	9.0	25
830	b	b	2195	10.3	33
831	b	b	2378	10.5	35
832	b	b	2636	10.7	38
834	b	b	1905	8.7	23
835	b	b	1926	8.9	24
840	b	b	1250	5.9	4
841	b	b	2642	9.7	32
842	b	b	2506	11.1	39

APPENDIX E

Three-Digit Occupation Code	Three-Digit Industry Code	Class of Worker	Income Median ($)	Education Median (years)	Bose Index
843	b	b	2686	12.1	46
850	b	b	5017	12.3	58
851	b	b	3462	11.8	48
852	b	b	4475	12.4	56
853	b	2	4299	12.3	54
853	b	1	3041	12.1	47
853	b	Not 1, 2	3871	12.3	62
854	b	b	3648	12.3	51
860	b	b	1398	11.2	34
874	b	b	1000	10.8	30
875	b	b	1777	10.6	33
890	b	b	1722	9.7	28
901	b	b	3738	10.7	43
902	b	b	899	7.5	11
903	b	b	668	9.1	19
905	b	b	NA	8.8	NA
960	b	b	2500	9.0	27
962	b	b	2250	8.7	25
963	b	b	2000	9.5	28
964	b	b	1866	8.9	24
965	b	b	5950	9.5	47
970	b	b	598	8.3	14
971	b	b	NA	4.2	NA
972	b	b	2525	9.4	30
973	b	b	3752	10.5	42
985	016-156	b	2121	10.4	33
985	196	b	2699	8.7	27
985	206	b	2121	10.4	33
985	207	b	2819	9.7	33
985	208	b	2361	9.5	30
985	209	b	2954	8.9	29
985	216	b	3553	9.7	36
985	217	b	2331	9.0	27
985	218	b	2845	10.3	36
985	219	b	2592	9.2	29
985	236	b	4253	9.9	41
985	237	b	4242	8.7	34
985	238	b	3831	9.5	37
985	239	b	3892	10.0	40
985	246	b	3685	10.1	39
985	247	b	3756	9.0	33
985	248	b	3453	9.5	35

Three-Digit Occupation Code	Three-Digit Industry Code	Class of Worker	Income Median ($)	Education Median (years)	Bose Index
985	249	b	NA	13.1	NA
985	256	b	4407	8.8	36
985	257	b	2756	7.9	23
985	258	b	3738	11.9	49
985	259	b	3490	10.2	39
985	267	b	4418	9.2	38
985	268	b	4238	9.6	39
985	269	b	4512	8.9	37
985	276	b	3500	9.5	35
985	286	b	2692	11.3	42
985	287	b	2500	10.5	36
985	289	b	3500	10.1	38
985	296	b	2960	8.9	29
985	306	b	3536	8.7	31
985	307	b	3114	9.9	35
985	308	b	2807	8.6	27
985	309	b	2652	10.5	36
985	316	b	2705	9.5	31
985	317	b	2623	8.6	26
985	318	b	3508	9.3	34
985	319	b	3136	8.0	25
985	326	b	3500	7.2	22
985	329	b	2607	7.9	22
985	346–348	b	2783	8.8	28
985	349	b	2649	8.2	24
985	356	b	2783	8.8	28
985	359–367	b	2581	9.7	32
985	386	b	3576	10.0	38
985	387	b	3307	9.4	34
985	389	b	2883	10.0	35
985	396–398	b	2780	10.5	37
985	406	b	4000	10.0	40
985	407	b	2750	9.8	33
985	408	b	1976	8.6	23
985	409	b	2907	9.4	32
985	416	b	5025	10.6	48
985	419	b	3000	12.0	46
985	426–429	b	3812	9.8	38
985	436–438	b	2727	9.0	29
985	459	b	2262	9.0	26
985	506	b	4093	8.2	31
985	507–526	b	4043	8.8	34

APPENDIX E

Three-Digit Occupation Code	Three-Digit Industry Code	Class of Worker	Income Median ($)	Education Median (years)	Bose Index
985	536-579	b	3508	10.6	41
985	606-696	b	2168	10.4	34
985	706-736	b	2121	10.4	33
985	806-809	b	2625	10.2	35
985	816-839	b	1768	8.8	23
985	846-849	b	2121	10.4	33
985	867-898	b	2121	10.4	33
985	906-936	b	3925	11.2	46
985	998	b	2121	10.4	33
985	999, NA	b	2863	9.5	32
995	b	b	NA	NA	NA
NA	b	b	NA	NA	NA

[a]This table is based on the one presented in the codebook for the National Longitudinal Surveys (NLS) dataset and is available through the Center for Human Resource Research, Ohio State University, Worthington, Ohio.

The Bose scores developed by the NLS are intended for female incumbents only. The index was developed to be used in association with the occupations held by respondents in the NLS young and older women's cohorts. It was created using the relationship between 1959 median women's earnings, the 1960 median years of school completed by the experienced civilian female labor force, and the mixed-gender, female incumbent treatment prestige for the sampled jobs herein (n = 108). The resultant equation,

$$\text{Bose}(I) = -34.4 + 0.0048\,X(I) + 5.54\,Y(I),$$

where $X(I)$ is the median female earnings in 1959 and $Y(I)$ is the median female years of school completed in the ith three-digit census occupation, was then used to estimate prestige scores for the three-digit 1960 census occupations with female incumbents.

[b]Industry and/or class of worker is irrelevant for assigning median income, median education, and Bose index for this occupation.

Source: Income and education data sources are U.S. Bureau of the Census (1963, Table 9, pp. 123-29, and Table 30, pp. 406-15).

1970 BOSE INDEX[a]

Three-Digit Occupation Census Code	Male Scores		Female Scores	
	All Workers	Full Year	All Workers	Full Year
Professional, technical, and kindred				
1 Accountants	76	76	56	55
2 Architects	86	86	86	85
3 Computer programmers	67	67	83	82
4 Computer systems analysts	80	80	82	81
5 Computer specialists, not elsewhere classified	80	79	69	68
Engineers				
6 aeronautical/astronautical	88	87	90	89
10 chemical	88	87	98	96
11 civil	82	81	92	90
12 electrical & electronic	83	83	89	87
13 industrial	77	76	72	70
14 mechanical	83	83	98	96
15 metallurgical	85	85	NA	NA
20 mining	80	80	NA	NA
21 petroleum	85	85	NA	NA
22 sales	82	82	100[b]	100[b]
23 not elsewhere classified	81	81	91	90
24 Farm management advisors	80	79	82	81
25 Foresters & conservationists	55	55	40	40
26 Home management advisors	NA	NA	84	83
30 Judges	100[b]	100[b]	75	74
31 Lawyers	100[b]	100[b]	95	94
32 Librarians	72	72	80	81
33 Archivists & curators	65	65	74	74
34 Actuaries	91	91	76	75
35 Mathematicians	89	89	90	88
36 Statisticians	78	77	70	69
Life and physical scientists				
42 agricultural	75	74	47	47
43 atmospheric & space	85	84	53	52
44 biological	80	79	84	83
45 chemists	81	80	89	88
51 geologists	88	87	78	80
52 marine	86	86	NA	NA
53 physicists & astronomers	92	91	96	95
54 not elsewhere classified	89	88	NA	NA
55 Operations & systems research & analysts	69	69	75	74

	Three-Digit Occupation Census Code	Male Scores		Female Scores	
		All Workers	Full Year	All Workers	Full Year
56	Personnel & labor relations	73	73	60	60
	Physicians & related				
61	chiropractors	82	82	67	67
62	dentists	100[b]	100[b]	76	76
63	optometrists	97	97	83	82
64	pharmacists	81	81	76	76
65	physicians, medical & osteopathic	100[b]	100[b]	99	98
71	podiatrists	91	90	69	68
72	veterinarians	95	95	80	79
73	health practitioners, not elsewhere classified	71	70	NA	NA
74	Dietician	45	44	50	50
75	Registered nurses	52	51	58	57
76	Therapists	67	67	75	74
	Health technologists/technicians				
80	clinical lab	59	58	65	65
81	dental hygienicists	66	66	68	68
82	health record technologists & technicians	54	54	62	62
83	radiologic technologists & technicians	52	52	52	51
84	therapy assistants	48	48	45	45
85	not elsewhere classified	57	57	50	49
86	Clergymen	68	68	46	46
90	Religious workers, not elsewhere classified	65	65	52	52
	Social scientists				
91	economists	86	86	82	81
92	political scientists	88	87	NA	NA
93	psychologists	86	85	93	93
94	sociologists	79	79	83	82
95	urban & regional planners	82	82	85	84
96	not elsewhere classified	80	80	78	77
100	Social workers	72	72	80	80
101	Recreation workers	56	55	46	47
	Teachers, college & university				
102	agriculture	85	85	NA	NA
103	atmospheric, earth, marine, space	83	83	66	68
104	biology	84	83	83	85
105	chemistry	85	85	87	87
110	physics	83	83	98	100
111	engineering	88	88	75	78
112	mathematics	80	80	82	87
113	health specialties	99	98	91	92
114	psychology	89	89	92	94
115	business & commerce	84	83	85	88
116	economics	86	85	94	97
120	history	80	80	83	87

	Three-Digit Occupation Census Code	Male Scores		Female Scores	
		All Workers	Full Year	All Workers	Full Year
	[Teachers, college & university]				
121	sociology	81	81	85	87
122	social science, not elsewhere classified	84	84	95	95
123	art, drama, music	80	81	78	82
124	coaches & physical education	80	79	87	93
125	education	89	89	96	97
126	English	79	80	86	90
130	foreign language	79	79	81	86
131	home economics	NA	NA	89	93
132	law	99	99	NA	NA
133	theology	77	77	71	74
134	trade, industrial, technical	77	77	69	70
135	miscellaneous college & university teachers	80	80	88	91
140	college & university teachers, subject unspecified	78	78	75	78
141	Adult education teachers	67	66	71	73
142	Elementary school teachers	73	74	82	88
143	Prekindergarten & kindergarten teachers	61	61	62	65
144	Secondary school teachers	76	76	84	89
145	Teachers exc. college & university, not elsewhere classified	53	53	48	50
	Engineering & science technicians				
150	agricultural & biological	48	48	50	49
151	chemical technicians	53	53	56	55
152	draftsmen	53	52	55	54
153	electrical & electronic engineering	54	54	56	56
154	industrial engineering	53	53	55	54
155	mechanical engineering	57	57	NA	NA
156	mathematical engineering	60	59	NA	NA
161	surveyors	48	48	39	42
162	not elsewhere classified	52	52	53	53
	Technicians exc. health, engineering, and science				
163	pilots	82	81	78	77
164	air traffic controllers	63	63	63	62
165	embalmers	54	54	NA	NA
170	flight engineers	66	66	NA	NA
171	radio operators	47	47	45	45
172	tool programmers, numerical control	60	60	78	78
173	not elsewhere classified	52	52	55	55
174	Vocational & educational counselors	79	78	91	94
	Writers & artists				
175	actors	56	62	58	74
180	athletes & kindred workers	46	46	37	40
181	authors	74	74	74	74

	Three-Digit Occupation Census Code	Male Scores All Workers	Male Scores Full Year	Female Scores All Workers	Female Scores Full Year
	[Writers & artists]				
182	dancers	42	43	42	47
183	designers	66	65	60	59
184	editors & reporters	75	75	72	71
185	musicians & composers	42	43	40	41
190	painters & sculptors	59	59	54	54
191	photographers	51	51	45	45
192	public relations & publicity writers	77	76	69	68
193	radio & television announcers	53	53	46	46
194	writers, artists, entertainers, not elsewhere classified	60	60	54	54
195	Research workers, not specified	77	77	75	74
196	Professional, technical, kindred allocated	60	60	60	60
	Managers and administrators, except farm				
201	Assessors, controllers, treasurers, local public admin.	50	50	48	48
202	Bank officers & financial managers	72	72	57	57
203	Buyers & shippers, farm products	48	48	NA	NA
205	Buyers, wholesale & retail trade	55	55	54	53
210	Credit men	60	60	52	52
211	Funeral directors	59	59	59	58
212	Health administrators	79	78	66	65
213	Construction inspectors, public admin.	52	51	NA	NA
215	Inspectors, exc. construction; public admin.	54	54	55	55
216	Managers & superintendents, building	47	47	40	40
220	Office managers, not elsewhere classified	60	60	59	58
221	Officers, pilots, pursers, ship	50	49	60	60
222	Officials & admin., public admin., not elsewhere classified	65	65	62	61
223	Officials of lodges, societies, unions	59	59	63	63
224	Postmasters & mail superintendents	55	55	58	57
225	Purchasing agents & buyers, not elsewhere classified	60	60	60	59
226	Railroad conductors	54	54	63	62
230	Restaurant, cafeteria, & bar managers	49	49	42	42
231	Sales managers & department heads, retail	54	53	49	48
233	Sales managers exc. retail trade	76	76	63	62
235	School admin., college	88	88	88	87
240	School admin., elementary & secondary	86	86	91	91

	Male Scores		Female Scores	
Three-Digit Occupation Census Code	All Workers	Full Year	All Workers	Full Year
245 Managers & admin., not elsewhere classified, salaried	61	61	54	54
247 Managers & admin., not elsewhere classified, self-employed	50	50	44	44
246 Managers & admin., exc. farm, allocated	51	51	49	48
Sales workers				
260 Advertising agents & salesmen	66	66	53	52
261 Auctioneers	52	51	NA	NA
262 Demonstrators	50	50	33	36
264 Hucksters & peddlers	41	41	31	32
265 Insurance agents, brokers, & underwriters	59	58	52	51
266 Newsboys	20	20	31	32
270 Real estate agents & brokers	58	58	48	48
271 Stock & bond salesmen	83	83	57	56
280 Salesmen & sales clerks, not elsewhere classified	50	49	36	36
Sales representatives				
281 manufacturing	63	62	44	44
282 wholesale	54	54	44	43
283 Sales clerks, retail	42	41	36	36
284 Salesmen, retail	48	48	40	40
285 Salesmen of services & construction	54	54	37	38
296 Sales workers, allocated	44	44	36	36
Clerical and kindred workers				
301 Bank tellers	44	44	47	47
303 Billing clerks	46	46	47	47
305 Bookkeepers	49	48	48	48
310 Cashiers	35	35	36	37
311 Clerical assistants, social welfare	NA	NA	46	45
312 Clerical supervisors, not elsewhere classified	58	58	60	59
313 Collectors, bill & account	46	46	46	46
314 Counter clerks, exc. food	42	41	40	40
315 Dispatchers & starters, vehicle	49	49	44	44
320 Enumerators & interviewers	45	46	35	41

	Male Scores		Female Scores	
Three-Digit Occupation Census Code	All Workers	Full Year	All Workers	Full Year
321 Estimators & investigators, not elsewhere classified	58	58	49	49
323 Expeditors & production controllers	51	51	52	51
325 File clerks	41	41	43	43
326 Insurance adjusters, examiners, investigators	66	66	53	53
330 Library attendants & assistants	39	40	40	41
331 Mail carriers, post office	49	49	48	48
332 Mail handlers, exc. post office	40	39	42	42
333 Messengers, telegraph, & office boys	30	30	36	38
334 Meter readers, utilities	44	44	47	46
Office machine operators				
341 bookkeeping/billing	45	45	47	47
342 calculating machine	46	46	48	48
343 computer & peripheral equipment	49	49	52	52
344 duplicating machine	41	41	46	45
345 keypunch	48	48	48	48
350 tabulating machine	45	45	51	50
355 not elsewhere classified	41	41	45	44
360 Payroll & timekeeping clerks	49	49	51	51
361 Postal clerks	50	49	54	53
362 Proofreaders	51	51	47	47
363 Real estate appraisers	69	69	56	55
364 Receptionists	41	41	43	43
Secretaries				
372 all	50	49	51	50
370 legal	54	53	53	53
371 medical	46	46	51	50
374 Shipping & receiving clerks	42	42	44	44
375 Statistical clerks	50	49	50	49
376 Stenographers	57	57	52	52
381 Stock clerks & storekeepers	43	42	46	45
382 Teacher aides, exc. school monitors	38	40	36	39
384 Telegraph operators	49	49	52	51
385 Telephone operators	45	44	46	46
390 Ticket, station, express agents	52	51	58	57
391 Typists	44	44	46	46
392 Weighers	41	41	38	38

	Male Scores		Female Scores	
Three-Digit Occupation Census Code	All Workers	Full Year	All Workers	Full Year
394 Miscellaneous clerical workers	50	49	47	47
395 Not specified clerical workers	46	45	46	46
396 Clerical & kindred workers, allocated	44	44	44	43
Craftsmen and kindred workers				
401 Automobile accessories installers	40	40	NA	NA
402 Bakers	35	35	32	32
413 Cabinet makers	36	36	32	33
420 Carpet installers	42	42	44	43
Construction crafts				
410 brick & stone masons	38	39	43	43
411 brick & stone mason apprentices	44	43	NA	NA
412 bulldozer operators	32	31	38	38
415 carpenters	37	37	42	43
416 carpenter apprentices	40	41	NA	NA
421 cement & concrete finishers	29	30	33	34
430 electricians	51	51	54	53
431 electrician apprentices	45	45	NA	NA
436 excavating, grading, road machine operators	35	35	40	39
440 floor layers, exc. tile setters	39	39	43	42
510 painters, construction & maintenance	32	32	41	41
511 painter apprentices	39	39	NA	NA
512 paper hangers	35	36	28	31
520 plasterers	36	36	54	55
521 plasterer apprentices	37	37	NA	NA
522 plumber & pipe fitter	48	48	56	55
523 plumber & pipe fitter apprentices	44	44	NA	NA
534 roofers & slaters	31	32	32	32
550 structural metal craftsmen	48	47	53	52
560 tile setters	40	40	33	32
424 Cranemen, derrickmen, & hoistmen	39	38	49	48
425 Decorators & window dressers	46	46	41	41
426 Dental laboratory technicians	48	48	46	46
433 Electric power linemen & cablemen	51	51	53	52
435 Engravers, exc. photoengravers	44	44	43	43
441 Foreman, not elsewhere classified	52	52	50	49
443 Furniture & wood finishers	33	32	31	31
444 Furriers	39	39	30	31
445 Glaziers	45	44	43	43
450 Inspectors, scalers, graders, log & lumber	35	34	32	32
452 Inspectors, not elsewhere classified	48	48	39	39

	Three-Digit Occupation Census Code	Male Scores		Female Scores	
		All Workers	Full Year	All Workers	Full Year
453	Jewelers & watchmakers	44	44	40	40
455	Locomotive engineers	55	55	76	74
456	Locomotive firemen	52	52	NA	NA
	Mechanics & repairmen				
470	air conditioning & heat	47	46	54	53
471	aircraft	51	51	57	56
472	automobile body repairmen	39	39	44	44
473	automobile mechanics	39	39	46	46
474	auto mechanic apprentices	33	33	NA	NA
475	data-processing machine repair	56	55	53	52
480	farm implements	38	38	NA	NA
481	heavy equipment mechanics	44	44	48	47
482	household appliance installer & repair	45	45	45	45
483	loom fixers	26	26	NA	NA
484	office machine	48	48	53	52
485	radio & television	47	46	47	47
486	railroad & car shop	40	40	56	56
491	mechanics, exc. auto, apprentices	46	46	NA	NA
492	miscellaneous mechanics & repair, apprentices	46	46	50	49
495	not specified mechanics & repair	45	45	44	44
	Metal craftsmen, exc. mechanics				
403	blacksmith	35	34	NA	NA
404	boilermaker	44	43	NA	NA
442	forgemen & hammermen	40	40	39	38
446	heat treaters, annealers, temperers	42	41	47	46
454	job & die setters	43	43	46	46
461	machinists	47	47	43	43
462	machinist apprentices	43	43	NA	NA
502	millwrights	48	48	66	65
503	molders, metal	36	35	38	38
504	molder apprentices	42	42	NA	NA
514	pattern & model makers	53	53	51	51
533	rollers & finishers	42	42	39	39
535	sheetmetal workers & tinsmiths	48	48	48	47
536	sheetmetal apprentices	44	44	NA	NA
540	ship fitters	45	45	NA	NA
561	tool & die makers	53	53	51	50
562	tool & die maker apprentices	47	47	NA	NA
501	Millers, grain, flour, feed	26	26	NA	NA
505	Motion picture projectionists	42	41	37	40
506	Opticians, lens grinders, polishers	49	48	45	45
516	Piano & organ tuners & repairmen	42	42	NA	NA
525	Power station operators	53	52	51	51

		Male Scores		Female Scores	
Three-Digit Occupation Census Code		All Workers	Full Year	All Workers	Full Year
	Printing craftsmen				
405	book binders	46	46	38	38
422	compositors and typesetters	49	48	44	44
423	printing trades apprentices & pressman	40	40	NA	NA
434	electrotypers & stereotypers	51	51	NA	NA
515	photoengravers & lithographers	54	54	49	48
530	pressmen & plate printers	48	48	45	45
531	pressman apprentices	45	45	NA	NA
542	Shoe repairmen	22	22	29	29
543	Sign painters & letterers	42	41	36	36
545	Stationary engineers	48	48	54	53
546	Stone cutters & carvers	33	32	29	29
551	Tailors	31	31	31	30
552	Telephone installers & repairmen	51	51	55	54
554	Telephone linemen & splicers	48	48	57	56
563	Upholsterers	33	33	34	34
575	Craftsmen & kindred workers, not elsewhere classified	43	42	39	39
580	Former members of the armed forces	37	36	38	38
586	Craftsmen & kindred workers, allocated	38	38	35	35
	Operatives, except transport				
601	Asbestos & insulation workers	48	48	39	39
602	Assemblers	43	43	41	41
603	Blasters and powdermen	32	31	NA	NA
604	Bottling & canning operatives	35	35	24	29
605	Chainmen, rodmen, axmen, surveying	39	39	NA	NA
610	Checkers, examiners, inspectors, mfg.	47	47	40	40
611	Clothing ironers & pressers	26	26	24	24
612	Cutting operatives, not elsewhere classified	36	35	29	29
613	Dressmakers & seamstresses, exc. factory	27	26	29	29
614	Drillers, earth	38	38	37	37
615	Dry wall installers & lathers	41	41	38	37
620	Dyers	30	29	34	34
623	Garage workers & gas station attendants	27	28	29	30
624	Graders & sorters, mfg.	32	32	28	30
625	Produce graders & packers, exc. factory & farm	16	17	19	24

		Male Scores		Female Scores	
Three-Digit Occupation Census Code		All Workers	Full Year	All Workers	Full Year
630	Laundry & drycleaning operatives, not elsewhere classified	30	30	25	25
631	Meat cutters & butchers, exc. mfg.	44	44	32	32
633	Meat cutters & butchers, mfg.	36	36	26	26
634	Meat wrappers, retail	29	29	40	40
	Metal operatives, exc. precision machine				
621	polisher, filer	32	31	32	32
622	furnacemen, smeltermen, pourers	38	37	41	41
626	heaters, metal	40	40	NA	NA
635	metal platers	39	39	43	42
656	punch & stamping press operative	39	38	37	36
660	riveters & fasteners	35	35	35	34
665	solderers	35	35	40	40
680	welders & fame cutters	40	39	41	40
636	Milliners	NA	NA	31	31
640	Mine operatives, not elsewhere classified	36	36	36	36
641	Mixing operatives	37	37	38	38
642	Oilers & greasers, exc. auto	36	36	34	34
643	Packers & wrappers, exc. meat & produce	33	33	33	33
644	Painters, manufactured articles	35	34	36	35
645	Photographic process workers	46	46	43	43
	Precision machine operatives				
650	drill press	40	40	37	37
651	grinding machine operatives	42	42	42	42
652	lathe & milling machine	46	46	43	42
653	not elsewhere classified	46	46	36	36
661	Sailors & deckhands	34	35	42	43
662	Sawyers	22	22	32	32
663	Sewers & stitchers	24	24	29	29
664	Shoemaking machine operatives	24	23	29	29
666	Stationary firemen	38	38	32	31
	Textile operatives				
670	carding & combing	18	18	27	27
671	knitters, loopers, toppers	30	29	30	30
672	spinners, twisters, winders	25	25	28	28
673	weavers	24	24	33	33
674	not elsewhere classified	26	26	31	31
681	Winding operatives, not elsewhere classified	45	45	40	40
690	Machine operatives, misc. specified	39	39	35	35
692	Machine operatives, not specified	40	40	37	36

Three-Digit Occupation Census Code	Male Scores		Female Scores	
	All Workers	Full Year	All Workers	Full Year
694 Miscellaneous operatives	38	38	33	34
695 Not specified operatives	39	39	34	33
696 Operatives, exc. transport, allocated	33	33	27	27
Transport equipment operatives				
701 Boatmen & canalmen	33	33	NA	NA
703 Bus drivers	39	39	34	37
704 Conductors & motormen, urban rail transit	49	48	NA	NA
705 Deliverymen & routemen	42	42	37	38
706 Forklift & tow motor operatives	35	35	44	43
710 Motormen: mine, factory, logging camp	29	28	NA	NA
711 Parking attendants	29	28	31	34
712 Railroad brakemen	50	49	48	48
713 Railroad switchmen	49	48	57	56
714 Taxicab drivers & chauffeurs	33	33	35	36
715 Truck drivers	36	36	43	42
726 Transport equipment operatives, allocated	33	33	36	36
Laborers, except farm				
740 Animal caretakers, exc. farm	31	30	34	35
750 Carpenters' helpers	23	24	29	30
751 Construction laborers, exc. carpenter's helpers	27	27	30	31
752 Fishmen & oystermen	24	24	21	24
753 Freight & material handlers	34	34	35	35
754 Garbage collectors	24	23	31	30
755 Gardeners & groundskeepers, exc. farm	23	22	23	25
760 Longshoremen & stevedores	34	33	44	44
761 Lumbermen, raftsmen, woodchoppers	18	18	24	25
762 Stock handlers	27	27	34	34
763 Teamsters	23	23	NA	NA
764 Vehicle washers & equipment cleaners	26	26	26	27
770 Warehousemen, not elsewhere classified	42	42	46	45
780 Miscellaneous laborers	28	28	29	30
785 Not specified laborers	28	27	28	29
796 Laborers, exc. farm, allocated	24	24	25	25

	Three-Digit Occupation Census Code	Male Scores		Female Scores	
		All Workers	Full Year	All Workers	Full Year
	Farmers and farm managers				
801	Farmers, owners & tenants	31	30	31	31
802	Farm managers	43	43	38	38
806	Farmers & farm managers, allocated	27	26	31	31
	Farm laborers and farm foremen				
821	Farm foremen	33	32	41	41
	Farm laborers				
822	wage workers	14	14	10	14
823	unpaid family workers	22	21	28	28
824	Farm service laborers, self-employed	36	36	34	36
846	Farm laborers & farm foremen, allocated	13	13	12	14
	Service workers, except private household				
	Cleaning service				
901	chambermaids & maids	22	22	20	21
902	cleaners & charwomen	24	24	20	20
903	janitors & sextons	26	26	22	22
	Food service				
910	bartenders	40	40	36	36
911	busboys	21	23	22	25
912	cooks, exc. private household	30	30	25	27
913	dishwashers	20	22	18	20
914	food counter & fountain workers	24	25	28	30
915	waiters	31	32	29	31
916	not elsewhere classified	24	24	26	28
	Health service				
921	dental assistants	39	39	43	43
922	health aides, exc. nursing	38	38	42	42
923	health trainees	34	34	37	41
924	lay midwives	NA	NA	38	38
925	nursing aides, orderlies, attendants	38	37	37	37
926	practical nurses	42	42	46	46
	Personal service				
931	airline stewardess	51	51	64	64
932	attendants, recreation & amusement	30	31	30	33
933	attendants, personal service, not elsewhere classified	35	35	37	38
934	baggage porters & bellhops	33	33	NA	NA
935	barbers	37	37	40	40
940	boarding & lodging housekeepers	37	37	32	32
941	bootblacks	8	8	NA	NA
942	child care workers, exc. private household	37	36	31	32
943	elevator operators	22	22	31	31
944	hairdressers & cosmetologists	44	44	40	40

	Three-Digit Occupation Census Code	Male Scores		Female Scores	
		All Workers	Full Year	All Workers	Full Year
	[Personal service]				
945	personal service apprentices	34	33	25	26
950	housekeepers exc. private household	43	43	39	39
952	school monitors	33	34	30	32
953	ushers, recreation & amusement	22	24	27	32
954	welfare service aides	43	43	40	40
	Protective service				
960	crossing guard, bridge tender	16	17	31	34
961	firemen, fire protection	52	52	63	62
962	guards & watchmen	37	36	42	42
963	marshals & constables	45	45	NA	NA
964	police & detectives	52	52	49	49
965	sheriffs & bailiffs	46	46	52	51
976	Service workers, allocated	28	28	28	28
	Private household workers				
980	Child care worker, private household	19	22	20	23
981	Cook	23	22	12	12
982	Housekeeper	22	21	12	12
983	Laundress	21	21	8	9
984	Maid & servant	13	13	10	11
986	Private household workers, allocated	17	17	6	6
	Mean ($\bar{X}$)	49.4	49.8	39.5	44.3

NA, Income and/or education data to project scores are not available from census tables. Individual respondents' income and education information can be used to project scores using the equations below.

[a]This index was constructed using the relationship between mixed-gender, female (male) incumbent prestige scores for the 108 sampled occupations herein and the 1970 median school years completed and median dollars earned of the female (male) experienced civilian labor force. (Education of 17+ years was coded as 17.0.) Scores were created separately for all workers and for full-year workers. The latter scores were constructed by multiplying income by the fraction 50.0/median weeks worked.

The resultant four equations are:

Bose Index (Male Workers) = 5.40(Median Years Male Education) + 0.0026(Median Dollars Male Income) − 39.6

Bose Index (Full-Year Male) = 5.37(Median Years Male Education) + 0.0026(Median Dollars Male Income)(50.0/Median Weeks Worked) − 39.5

Bose Index (Female Workers) = 5.97(Median Years Female Education) + 0.0046(Median Dollars Female Income) − 47.3

Bose Index (Full-Year Female) = 5.95(Median Years Female Education) + 0.0044(Median Dollars Female Income)(50.0/Median Weeks Worked) − 46.5

Over all census occupations, the median values were the following:

	Three-Digit Occupations Used Above (Mean Values)	Total Labor Force Age 16 and Over
Male Median Education	12.8	12.3
Male Median Earnings	$7,999	$7,620
Male Median Weeks Worked	49	50
Female Median Education	12.6	12.4
Female Median Earnings	$4,686	$3,646
Female Median Weeks Worked	48	50

[b] Actual projected scores for occupation nos. 22, 30, 31, 62, and 65 were 107, 108, 101, 109, and 117, respectively. Because of their large income figures, the female and male Bose index scores were "off scale." They have been rounded down to 100, which is the top of the prestige and socioeconomic index scales.

Source: Income and education data source is U.S. Bureau of the Census (1973, Table 1, pp. 1-11).

x   x   x   x   x

Three-Digit Occupation Census Code	Male Scores		Female Scores	
	All Workers	Full Year	All Workers	Full Year
I. Managerial and Professional Specialty Occupations				
Executive, Administrative, Managerial				
3 Legislators	73	74	69	74
4 Chief executives & gen'l admin., public admin.	50	48	56	55
5 Admin. & officials, public admin.	70	67	62	60
6 Admin., protective services	49	46	49	44
7 Financial managers	76	72	61	56
8 Personnel & labor relations managers	71	68	58	55
9 Purchasing managers	71	68	64	60
13 Managers, marketing, advertising, public relations	73	70	59	58
14 Admin., education & related fields	84	80	80	77
15 Managers, medicine & health	76	73	72	68
16 Managers, properties & real estate	54	53	45	45
17 Postmasters & mail superintendents	53	50	58	57
18 Funeral directors	57	55	58	58

	Three-Digit Occupation Census Code	Male Scores		Female Scores	
		All Workers	Full Year	All Workers	Full Year
19	Managers & admin., not elsewhere classified	67	65	54	53
	Management-related occupations				
23	accountants & auditors	69	67	62	59
24	underwriters	69	66	53	49
25	other financial officers	72	70	53	52
26	management analysts	79	79	79	78
27	personnel, training, & labor relations	62	60	62	59
28	purchasing agents & buyers	48	47	46	47
29	buyers, wholesale & retail	55	53	54	52
33	purchasing agents & buyers, not elsewhere classified	56	54	55	51
34	business & promotion agents	55	55	62	62
35	construction inspectors	45	43	51	50
36	inspectors & compliance officers	53	50	57	56
37	not elsewhere classified	69	67	64	61
	Professional Specialty Occupations				
43	Architects	78	77	76	77
	Engineers				
44	aerospace	78	75	87	84
45	metallurgical & materials	75	72	77	77
46	mining	75	73	71	75
47	petroleum	81	80	85	89
48	chemical	79	76	83	86
49	nuclear	78	75	83	82
53	civil	74	71	77	78
54	agricultural	74	72	100[b]	100[b]
55	electrical & electronic	73	70	78	75
56	industrial	67	63	60	57
57	mechanical	73	70	83	82
58	marine, naval architects	66	64	71	67
59	not elsewhere classified	74	72	81	79
63	Surveyors & mapping scientists	48	47	48	51
	Math & computer scientists				
64	systems analysts	71	68	86	81
65	operations & systems researchers	71	68	81	75
66	actuaries	84	82	85	80
67	statisticians	71	69	71	68
68	not elsewhere classified	85	82	93	91
	Natural scientists				
69	physicists & astronomers	88	85	90	87
73	chemists	72	70	82	79
74	atmospheric & space	71	69	62	64
75	geologists & geodesists	83	82	78	80
76	physical scientists, not elsewhere classified	75	73	78	77
77	agricultural & food	66	64	60	61

	Three-Digit Occupation Census Code	Male Scores		Female Scores	
		All Workers	Full Year	All Workers	Full Year
	[Natural scientists]				
78	biological & life	75	73	78	76
79	forestry & conservation	62	60	62	66
83	medical	100[b]	100[b]	84	82
	Health diagnosis				
84	physicians	100[b]	100[b]	100[b]	100[b]
85	dentists	100[b]	100[b]	80	83
86	veterinarians	97	94	81	80
87	optometrists	95	93	74	75
88	podiatrists	99	99	55	61
89	not elsewhere classified	89	89	69	69
	Health assessment				
95	registered nurses	60	59	65	65
96	pharmacists	76	74	81	83
97	dieticians	47	46	64	62
98	inhalation therapists	50	48	52	50
99	occupational therapists	59	56	71	69
103	physical therapists	69	68	72	72
104	speech therapists	77	76	81	79
105	therapists, not elsewhere classified	59	56	64	62
106	physicians' assistants	49	47	44	43
	Postsecondary teachers				
113	earth & marine science	80	83	66	65
114	biology	81	81	80	87
115	chemistry	78	81	69	78
116	physics	80	83	77	86
117	natural science, not elsewhere classified	79	78	76	93
118	psychology	87	86	89	94
119	economics	85	89	81	84
123	history	82	80	85	85
124	political science	79	78	88	97
125	sociology	81	80	91	97
126	social science, not elsewhere classified	79	78	82	86
127	engineering	76	77	69	76
128	mathematical science	74	78	71	83
129	computer science	61	65	62	72
133	medical science	100[b]	100[b]	95	99
134	health specialties	79	81	86	86
135	business & marketing	80	83	75	79
136	agriculture & forestry	81	79	65	68
137	art, drama, music	74	74	72	78
138	physical education	65	67	63	71
139	education	82	81	84	84
143	English	76	76	77	84
144	foreign language	72	75	72	80
145	law	99	100	100	100[b]
146	social work	82	78	97	100
147	theology	78	76	82	73
148	trade & industry	60	58	73	73

	Three-Digit Occupation Census Code	Male Scores		Female Scores	
		All Workers	Full Year	All Workers	Full Year
	[Postsecondary teachers]				
149	home economics	58	55	79	83
153	not elsewhere classified	74	74	69	74
154	subject not specified	81	82	82	88
	Teachers				
155	prekindergarten & kindergarten	56	56	51	50
156	elementary school	71	67	74	70
157	secondary school	71	68	74	71
158	special education	63	62	63	61
159	not elsewhere classified	55	56	54	61
163	Counselors, educational & vocational	70	68	79	76
164	Librarians	64	65	70	70
165	Archivists & curators	64	63	67	68
	Social scientists				
166	economists	80	79	80	77
167	psychologists	83	80	90	87
168	sociologists	80	82	85	84
169	not elsewhere classified	73	73	70	74
173	urban planners	76	73	88	84
174	Social workers	61	59	70	67
175	Recreation workers	46	49	41	42
176	Clergy	64	60	62	59
177	Religious workers, not elsewhere classified	57	55	54	54
178	Lawyers	100[b]	100[b]	96	99
179	Judges	95	93	78	78
	Writers, artists, entertainers				
183	author	67	69	65	70
184	technical writers	66	64	76	75
185	designers	57	56	50	53
186	musicians & composers	45	48	51	60
187	actors & directors	73	75	75	80
188	painters, sculptors, craft artists, printmakers	53	52	54	55
189	photographers	49	48	46	48
193	dancers	43	46	41	44
194	artists, performers, not elsewhere classified	45	47	45	47
195	editors & reporters	65	65	69	70
197	public relations specialists	70	69	70	70
198	announcers	48	49	57	61
199	athletes	52	52	47	50

		Male Scores		Female Scores	
	Three-Digit Occupation Census Code	All Workers	Full Year	All Workers	Full Year

II. Technical, Sales, and Administrative Support

   Technicians and Related Support

      Health technologists & technicians

203	clinical lab	56	55	64	62
204	dental hygienicists	61	62	63	62
205	health record technologists & technicians	56	55	58	55
206	radiologic technicians	51	48	55	53
207	licensed practical nurses	42	40	45	44
208	not elsewhere classified	50	49	47	45

      Technologists & technicians, exc. health

213	electrical & electronic	49	47	52	49
214	industrial engineering	48	46	52	49
215	mechanical engineering	54	52	51	52
216	engineering technicians, not elsewhere classified	52	50	52	52
217	draft occ.	48	47	53	53
218	surveying & mapping	42	41	43	50
223	biological technicians	47	46	48	48
224	chemical technicians	51	50	58	57
225	science technicians, not elsewhere classified	48	49	46	51
226	airplane pilots & navigators	84	78	78	72
227	air traffic controllers	60	58	55	55
228	broadcast equipment op.	44	43	44	43
229	computer programmers	62	61	72	70
233	tool programmers, numerical control	57	54	67	64
234	legal assistants	59	59	55	53
235	technicians, not elsewhere classified	56	56	63	64

   Sales Occupations

243	Supervisors & proprietors, sales occ.	50	48	46	44

      Sales representatives

253	insurance sales	67	65	53	50
254	real estate sales	65	65	57	61
255	securities & financial service sales	89	87	69	68
256	advertising	63	63	60	60
257	sales occ., other business services	59	59	50	52

      Nonretail commodity, sales

258	sales engineers	76	73	60	59
259	sales rep., mining, mfg., wholesale	59	57	50	52

      Retail & personal sales

263	motor vehicles & boats	45	44	44	46
264	apparel	38	40	32	35
265	shoes	35	38	33	36
266	furniture & home furnishings	43	42	40	44
267	radio, TV, appliances	43	44	39	42
268	hardware & building supplies	39	40	35	36

		Male Scores		Female Scores	
Three-Digit Occupation Census Code		All Workers	Full Year	All Workers	Full Year
	[Retail & personal sales]				
269	parts	40	39	42	41
274	sales, other commodities	39	42	33	36
275	sales counter clerks	39	40	34	35
276	cashiers	35	37	34	37
277	street and door-to-door sales	43	46	31	41
278	news vendors	33	38	32	39
283	Demonstrators, promoters, & models	43	44	31	41
284	Auctioneers	50	49	44	46
285	Sales support occ., not elsewhere classified	48	45	41	41
Administrative Support, Including Clerical					
	Supervisors				
303	general office	53	51	54	50
304	computer equipment op.	62	58	63	58
305	financial records processing	70	66	59	53
306	chief communications op.	57	54	71	64
307	distribution, scheduling, adjusting	47	45	55	51
308	Computer op.	47	46	47	44
309	Peripheral equipment op.	42	41	45	43
313	Secretaries	47	50	45	44
314	Stenographers	59	58	51	49
315	Typists	36	37	40	40
	Information clerks				
316	interviewers	45	49	39	42
317	hotel clerks	35	35	36	35
318	transportation ticket & reservation agents	49	47	58	57
319	receptionists	39	42	38	38
323	not elsewhere classified	42	45	40	43
	Records processing, exc. financial				
325	classified ad	53	52	43	43
326	correspondence clerks	53	50	49	46
327	order clerks	41	40	46	45
328	personnel clerks, exc. payroll	48	48	46	44
329	library clerks	38	42	39	44
335	file clerks	39	40	37	39
336	records clerks	44	44	43	42
	Financial records				
337	bookkeepers, accounting	47	47	44	43
338	payroll & timekeeping clerks	44	42	47	44
339	billing clerks	41	40	43	42
343	cost & rate clerks	51	50	46	43
344	billing, posting, calculating machine op.	39	39	41	39
345	Duplicating machine op.	37	37	40	41

	Male Scores		Female Scores	
Three-Digit Occupation Census Code	All Workers	Full Year	All Workers	Full Year
346 Mail-preparing & paper-handling op.	37	37	36	37
347 Office machine op., not elsewhere classified	36	36	39	39
348 Telephone op.	39	40	43	42
349 Telegraphers	47	46	48	48
353 Communications equipment op., not elsewhere classified	45	45	35	36
354 Postal clerks, exc. mail carriers	47	45	59	60
355 Mail carriers, postal service	47	44	53	57
356 Mail clerks, exc. postal service	35	36	38	40
357 Messengers	32	33	36	39
Material recording & scheduling				
359 dispatchers	45	44	47	46
363 production coordinators	46	44	48	46
364 traffic, shipping, receiving clerks	37	36	42	40
365 stock & inventory clerks	38	38	43	42
366 meter readers	39	37	46	46
368 weighers, measurers, checkers	40	39	39	40
369 samplers	40	38	43	43
373 expediters	43	42	45	44
374 not elsewhere classified	43	45	38	39
375 Insurance adjusters, examiners, & investigators	62	59	49	45
376 Investigators & adjusters, exc. insurance	57	55	50	48
377 Eligibility clerks, social welfare	54	51	58	53
378 Bill & account collectors	42	41	44	42
Miscellaneous admin. support				
379 general office clerks	40	41	42	42
383 bank tellers	39	39	39	37
384 proofreaders	47	48	41	43
385 data-entry keyers	41	41	44	42
386 statistical clerks	48	47	47	46
387 teachers' aides	40	44	33	34
389 not elsewhere classified	53	52	47	46
III. Service Occupations				
Private Household				
403 Launderers & ironers	35	32	20	21
404 Cooks, private household	27	25	21	22
405 Housekeepers & butlers	28	27	19	19
406 Child care workers, private household	26	29	25	25
407 Private household cleaners & servants	24	24	15	16

		Male Scores		Female Scores	
Three-Digit Occupation Census Code		All Workers	Full Year	All Workers	Full Year

Protective Service
    Supervisors

413	firefighting	54	50	59	59
414	police & detectives	57	54	60	58
415	guards	45	44	48	47
416	Fire inspection & prevention	45	43	41	44
417	Firefighting	47	44	48	51
418	Police & detectives, public service	51	48	60	57
423	Sheriffs, bailiffs, other law enforcement	44	41	51	48
424	Correctional institution officers	42	39	50	48
425	Crossing guards	20	29	26	36
426	Guards & police, exc. public service	36	36	39	42
427	Protective service occ., not elsewhere classified	33	36	31	41

Service Occupations, Except Protective and Household
    Food prep. & service

433	supervisors	39	39	37	39
434	bartenders	34	34	34	34
435	waiters & waitresses	33	33	30	31
436	cooks, exc. short order	30	31	30	31
437	short-order cooks	28	30	30	31
438	food counter, fountain, & related occ.	29	32	28	32
439	kitchen workers	30	32	31	33
443	waiters'/waitresses' assistants	26	27	28	33
444	misc. food preparation occ.	26	27	28	32

    Health service

445	dental assistants	51	52	39	38
446	health aides, exc. nursing	37	37	39	38
447	nursing aides, orderlies, attendants	36	35	37	36

    Cleaning & building service

448	supervisors	41	39	40	37
449	maids & housemen	29	28	25	26
453	janitors & cleaners	32	32	29	32
454	elevator op.	29	28	38	37
455	pest control occ.	37	36	39	39

    Personal service

456	supervisors	43	43	48	45
457	barbers	35	33	40	40
458	hairdressers & cosmetologists	39	38	37	38
459	amusement & recreation attendants	34	37	36	41
463	guides	37	40	36	42
464	ushers	29	37	34	45
465	public transportation attendants	47	45	67	63

	Three-Digit Occupation Census Code	Male Scores		Female Scores	
		All Workers	Full Year	All Workers	Full Year
	[Personal service]				
466	baggage porters & bellhops	33	33	41	40
467	welfare service aides	44	44	34	35
468	child care workers, exc. private household	35	37	30	31
469	not elsewhere classified	34	34	33	34
IV.	Farming, Forestry, and Fishing				
	Farm operators & managers				
473	farmers	39	36	36	33
474	horticultural specialty farmers	41	39	35	34
475	managers, farms, exc. horticultural	45	43	43	42
476	managers, horticultural specialty farms	37	38	36	39
477	Supervisors, farm workers	40	39	44	45
479	Farm workers	23	23	26	27
483	Marine life cultivation workers	34	34	37	37
484	Nursery workers	29	30	31	32
485	Supervisors, related agricultural occ.	41	39	40	42
486	Groundskeepers & gardeners, exc. farm	31	32	33	35
487	Animal caretakers, exc. farm	34	34	35	36
488	Graders & sorters, agricultural products	18	20	18	19
489	Inspectors, agricultural products	38	39	36	37
	Forestry & logging				
494	supervisors	47	46	45	46
495	forestry workers	34	36	34	39
496	timber cutting & logging	33	33	37	37
497	Captains & other officers, fishing vessels	47	47	52	62
498	Fishers	39	38	36	36
499	Hunters & trappers	42	42	43	49
V.	Precision Production, Craft, and Repair				
503	Supervisors, mechanics & repairers	49	47	56	55
505	Automobile mechanics	38	37	45	45
506	Automobile mechanic apprentices	37	37	50	65
507	Bus, truck, & stationary engine mechanics	41	39	50	52
508	Aircraft engine mechanics	48	46	56	54
509	Small engine repairers	35	35	41	41
514	Automobile body & related repairers	38	36	44	44
515	Aircraft mechanics, exc. engine	46	45	55	52
516	Heavy equipment mechanics	43	41	54	54

		Male Scores		Female Scores	
Three-Digit Occupation Census Code		All Workers	Full Year	All Workers	Full Year
517	Farm equipment mechanics	38	36	45	46
518	Industrial machinery repairers	42	40	47	44
519	Machinery maintenance occ.	42	41	46	47
523	Electronic repairers, commun. & industrial equipment	41	40	45	46
525	Data-processing equipment repairers	51	49	52	50
526	Household appliance & power tool repairers	40	38	46	43
527	Telephone line installers & repairers	48	45	60	57
529	Telephone installers & repairers	50	47	61	57
533	Misc. electrical & electronic equipment	43	41	48	46
534	Heating, air conditioning, & refrig. mechanics	42	40	48	47
535	Camera, watch, & musical instru. repairers	40	40	41	40
536	Locksmith & safe repairers	39	38	41	39
538	Office machine repairers	42	40	49	50
539	Mechanical controls & valve repairers	42	39	45	44
543	Elevator installers & repairers	49	48	50	47
544	Millwrights	48	46	47	46
547	Specified mechanics & repairers, not elsewhere classified	41	40	43	43
549	Not specified mechanics & repairers	42	40	46	45
	Construction supervisors				
553	brick & stone masons	47	47	35	21
554	carpenters & related workers	46	45	56	59
555	electricians & power transmission	54	52	59	57
556	painters, paper hangers, plasterers	45	44	45	52
557	plumbers, pipefitters, steamfitters	53	51	57	53
558	not elsewhere classified	51	50	59	58
	Construction trades				
563	brick & stone masons	37	38	41	45
564	brick & stone mason apprentices	34	35	45	47
565	tile setters, hard & soft	39	39	42	43
566	carpet installers	38	38	41	42
567	carpenters	37	37	40	42
569	carpenter apprentices	34	35	40	39
573	drywall installers	37	39	43	52
575	electricians	46	44	49	48
576	electrician apprentices	38	37	49	48
577	electrical power installers & repairers	47	45	52	53
579	painters, construction & maintenance	35	36	36	40
583	paper hanger	40	40	36	42

	Three-Digit Occupation Census Code	Male Scores		Female Scores	
		All Workers	Full Year	All Workers	Full Year
	[Construction trades]				
584	plasterers	37	37	37	43
585	plumbers, pipefitters, steamfitters	44	42	48	48
587	plumbers & pipefitter apprentices	37	36	46	42
588	concrete & terrazzo finishers	36	36	38	38
589	glaziers	40	38	38	38
593	insulation workers	39	40	41	46
594	paving, surfacing equipment op.	35	34	33	39
595	roofers	33	35	35	39
596	sheet metal duct installers	42	40	48	45
597	structural metal workers	42	42	49	49
598	drillers, earth	39	38	42	41
599	not elsewhere classified	36	36	40	44
	Extractive occ.				
613	supervisors	57	54	68	62
614	drillers, oil well	41	41	48	54
615	explosives workers	41	41	41	43
616	mining machine op.	43	42	51	52
617	not elsewhere classified	43	42	51	51
633	Supervisors, production occ.	49	47	50	47
	Precision metal working				
634	tool & die makers	48	45	52	49
635	tool & die maker apprentices	41	39	52	49
636	precision assemblers, metal	42	40	45	44
637	machinists	42	40	43	42
639	machinist apprentices	38	37	50	48
643	boilermakers	46	44	52	53
644	precision grinders, fitters, & tool sharpeners	44	42	49	48
645	pattern & model makers, metal	48	46	51	50
646	layout workers	41	39	48	49
647	precious stones & metal workers	39	38	36	37
649	engravers, metal	41	41	38	39
653	sheet metal workers	43	41	48	46
654	sheet metal worker apprentices	41	41	53	53
655	misc. precision metal workers	40	39	44	44
	Precision woodworking				
656	pattern makers	51	49	53	58
657	cabinet makers & bench carpenters	37	36	37	36
658	furniture & wood finishers	33	32	31	30
659	misc. precision woodworkers	40	39	40	39
	Precision textile, apparel, furnishings				
666	dressmakers	36	35	32	32
667	tailors	29	28	35	34
668	upholsterers	34	33	35	34
669	shoe repairers	29	27	34	31
673	apparel & fabric pattern makers	42	42	44	45
674	misc. precision apparel & fabric workers	38	37	34	34

		Male Scores		Female Scores	
	Three-Digit Occupation Census Code	All Workers	Full Year	All Workers	Full Year
	Precision workers, assorted materials				
675	hand molders	37	35	39	38
676	pattern makers, layout workers, cutters	44	43	44	46
677	optical goods workers	43	41	43	40
678	dental & medical appliance tech.	44	43	43	42
679	bookbinders	40	39	39	39
683	electrical & electronic assemblers	36	36	41	40
684	misc. precision workers, not elsewhere classified	39	38	41	39
686	Butchers & meat cutters	40	39	37	38
687	Bakers	37	36	35	36
688	Food batchmakers	35	34	34	35
689	Inspectors, testers, graders	45	43	46	44
693	Adjusters & calibrators	42	39	38	34
694	Water & sewage plant op.	40	38	49	51
695	Power plant op.	49	46	52	49
696	Stationary engineers	48	46	54	53
699	Misc. plant & system op.	46	43	55	50
VI.	Operators, Fabricators, and Laborers				
	Machine Operators, Assemblers, Inspectors				
	Metal & plastic working machine operatives				
703	lathe & turning setup operatives	42	39	51	46
704	lathe & turning machine operatives	42	40	46	44
705	milling & planing machine op.	42	40	45	42
706	punching & stamping press op.	39	37	42	40
707	rolling machine op.	47	45	43	41
708	drilling & boring machine operatives	40	39	42	41
709	grinding, abrading, buffing, polishing	38	38	42	41
713	forging machine op.	42	40	46	43
714	numerical control machine op.	46	44	50	48
715	misc. metal, plastic, stone, & glass op.	45	43	44	42
717	Fabricating machine op., not elsewhere classified	39	38	41	39
	Metal & plastic processing op.				
719	molding & casting	38	37	39	38
723	metal-plating machine op.	38	36	40	40
724	heat-treating equipment op.	44	42	46	45
725	misc. metal & plastic processing op.	36	35	40	38
	Woodworking machine op.				
726	wood lathe, etc.	37	35	42	40
727	sawing machine op.	31	30	37	35
728	shaping & joining machine op.	35	34	38	37
729	nailing & tacking machine op.	28	27	32	32
733	misc. woodworking machine op.	35	34	37	36

	Three-Digit Occupation Census Code	Male Scores		Female Scores	
		All Workers	Full Year	All Workers	Full Year
734	Printing machine op.	41	39	41	40
735	Photoengravers & lithographers	48	45	44	44
736	Typesetters & compositors	44	42	43	44
737	Misc. printing machine op.	40	39	39	39
	Textile & furnishing machine op.				
738	winding op.	30	28	32	30
739	knitting, looping, taping, & weaving op.	29	28	36	34
743	textile cutting machine op.	32	31	33	32
744	textile sewing machine op.	30	29	30	28
745	shoe machine op.	26	25	32	30
747	pressing machine op.	23	22	26	24
748	laundry & drycleaning machine op.	33	33	28	27
749	misc. textile machine op.	29	28	34	32
	Assorted materials machine op.				
753	cementing	36	36	38	37
754	packaging & filling machine op.	37	37	37	39
755	extruding & forming machine op.	39	37	41	40
756	mixing & blending machine op.	38	37	43	42
757	separating, filtering, clarifying	45	43	48	48
758	compressing & compacting machine op.	36	35	40	39
759	painting & paint spraying	37	36	39	38
763	roasting & baking machine op.	38	37	41	41
764	washing, cleaning, pickling	38	37	33	36
765	folding machine op.	35	34	33	33
766	furnace, kiln, & oven op. exc. food	42	41	48	48
768	crushing & grinding	38	36	40	41
769	slicing & cutting machine op.	36	35	36	35
773	motion picture projectionists	39	41	40	48
774	photographic process machine op.	40	40	40	41
777	misc. machine op., not elsewhere classified	40	38	40	39
779	machine op., not specified	38	37	40	38
783	Welders & cutters	40	39	44	42
784	Solderers & brazers	34	34	38	37
785	Assemblers	38	37	41	39
786	Handcutting & trimming occ.	36	36	29	30
787	Hand molding, casting, & forming occ.	36	35	36	35
789	Hand painting & decorating occ.	38	38	37	37
793	Hand engraving & printing occ.	39	39	40	40
794	Hand grinding & polishing occ.	33	33	37	36
795	Misc. hand working occ.	37	37	34	35
796	Production inspectors, checkers, examiners	43	41	43	41
797	Production testers	43	42	44	42

Three-Digit Occupation Census Code	Male Scores All Workers	Male Scores Full Year	Female Scores All Workers	Female Scores Full Year
798 Production samplers & weighers	38	37	39	37
799 Graders & sorters, exc. agricultural	35	35	30	33
Transportation and Material-Moving Occupations				
Motor vehicle op.				
803 supervisors	47	44	48	49
804 truck drivers, heavy	41	39	44	45
805 truck drivers, light	37	38	37	42
806 driver-sales workers	42	40	38	40
808 bus drivers	38	39	33	39
809 taxicab drivers & chauffeurs	34	34	36	38
813 parking lot attendants	30	31	33	35
814 motor transportation occ., not elsewhere classified	37	35	33	40
Rail transport				
823 conductors & yard masters	54	51	59	59
824 locomotive operating occ.	54	51	67	63
825 railroad brake, signal, & switch op.	48	47	58	59
826 rail vehicle op., not elsewhere classified	46	44	62	57
Water transport				
828 ship captain & mates	52	50	46	44
829 sailors & deckhands	39	40	46	54
833 marine engineers	43	42	54	53
834 bridge, lock, & lighthouse tenders	39	37	39	37
Material moving equip. op.				
843 supervisors	49	46	58	55
844 operating engineers	41	39	48	48
845 longshore equipment op.	44	45	41	46
848 hoist & winch op.	41	40	49	52
849 crane & tower op.	44	42	58	55
853 excavating & loading machine op.	41	39	45	46
855 grader, dozer, & scraper op.	36	34	43	43
856 industrial truck & tractor equip. op.	37	36	48	46
859 misc. material-moving op.	39	38	40	39
Handlers, Equipment Cleaners, Helpers, and Laborers				
863 Supervisors, handlers, cleaners, laborers, not elsewhere classified	48	45	51	49
Helpers				
864 mechanics & repairers	32	33	39	41
865 construction trades	31	32	36	39
866 surveyor	35	36	40	43
867 extractive occ.	38	39	48	48
869 Construction laborers	34	34	36	39
873 Production helpers	35	35	38	39
875 Garbage collectors	29	29	35	37

	Male Scores		Female Scores	
Three-Digit Occupation Census Code	All Workers	Full Year	All Workers	Full Year
876 Stevedores	42	44	46	53
877 Stock handlers & baggers	32	35	35	37
878 Machine feeders & offbearers	35	34	38	38
883 Freight, stock, & material handlers, not elsewhere classified	37	37	42	43
885 Garage & service station-related occ.	30	31	32	34
887 Vehicle washers & equipment cleaners	31	32	36	37
888 Hand packers & packagers	33	33	37	38
889 Laborers, exc. construction	35	35	37	37
Mean ($\bar{X}$)	49.3	48.4	50.3	50.7

[a]This index was constructed using the relationship between mixed-gender, female (male) incumbent prestige scores for the 108 sampled occupations herein and the 1980 median school years completed and mean dollars earned of the female (male) experienced civilian labor force. Scores were created separately for all workers and for year-round full-time workers.

The resultant four equations are:

Bose Index (Male Workers) = 4.84(Median Years Male Education) + 0.0013(Mean Dollars Male Income) − 38.1

Bose Index (Year-Round, Fulltime Male) = 4.58(Median Years Male Education) + 0.0013(Mean Dollars Male Fulltime Income) − 38.6

Bose Index (Female Workers) = 5.07 (Median Years Female Education) + 0.0028(Mean Dollars Female Income) − 44.0

Bose Index (Year-Round, Fulltime Female) = 4.49(Mean Years Female Education) + 0.0027(Mean Dollars Female Fulltime Income) − 42.4

Over all census occupations, the average values were the following:

	Three-Digit Occupations Used Above (Mean Values)	Total Labor Force Age 18 and Over
Male Median Education	13.8	12.7
Male Mean Earnings	$16,021	$16,929
Male Mean Year-Round, Full-time Earnings	$18,507	$19,943
Female Median Education	13.4	12.7
Female Mean Earnings	$9,421	$8,238
Female Mean Year-Round, Full-time Earnings	$12,206	$11,051

[b]Because of their large income figures, several Bose index scores, particularly for men, were "off scale." They have been rounded down to 100, which is the top of the prestige and socioeconomic index scales. The actual projected scores for occupation no. 54

were 120 and 154, for occupation no. 83 (104, 102), for occupation no. 84 (130, 129, 128, 128), for occupation no. 85 (115, 112), for occupation no. 133 (103), for occupation no. 145 (107), and for occupation no. 178 (104)

Source: Income and education data source is U.S. Bureau of the Census (1984, Table 1, pp. 1-252).

BIBLIOGRAPHY

Acker, Joan R. 1980. "Women and Stratification: A Review of the Literature." Contemporary Sociology 9:25-39.

Arnott, C., and V. Bengtson. 1970. "'Only a Homemaker': Distributive Justice and Role Choice Among Married Women." Sociology and Social Research 54:495-507.

Baudler, Lucille, and Donald Paterson. 1948. "Social Status of Women's Occupations." Occupations 26:421-24.

Blau, Peter, and Otis D. Duncan. 1967. The American Occupational Structure. New York: Wiley.

Bose, Christine E. 1980. "Social Status of the Homemaker." In Women and Household Labor, edited by Sarah F. Berk, pp. 69-87. Beverly Hills: Sage.

_____. 1973. Jobs and Gender: Sex and Occupational Prestige. Baltimore: The Johns Hopkins University Center for Metropolitan Planning and Research.

Bose, Christine E., and Peter H. Rossi. 1983. "Gender and Jobs: Prestige Standings of Occupations as Affected by Gender." American Sociological Review 48:316-30.

Boyd, Monica, and Hugh A. McRoberts. 1982. "Women, Men and Socioeconomic Indices: An Assessment." In Measures of Socioeconomic Status: Current Issues, edited by Mary Powers, pp. 129-59. Boulder: Westview Press.

Counts, George S. 1925. "The Social Status of Occupations: A Problem in Vocational Guidance." School Review 33:16-27.

Davis, Kingsley, and Wilbert Moore. 1945. "Some Principles of Stratification." American Sociological Review 10:242-49.

DeJong, Peter Y., Milton J. Brawer, and Stanley S. Robin. 1971. "Patterns of Female Intergenerational Occupational Mobility:

A Comparison with Male Patterns of Intergenerational Occupational Mobility." American Sociological Review 36:1033-42.

Dworkin, Rosalind. 1981. "Prestige Ranking of the Housewife Occupation." Sex Roles 7:59-63.

Ehrenreich, Barbara, and Dierdre English. 1975. "The Manufacture of Housework." Socialist Revolution 5:5-40.

Eichler, Margaret. 1976. "The Prestige of the Occupation Housewife." Paper presented at the Symposium on the Working Sexes, University of British Columbia, Vancouver, Canada.

England, Paula. 1979. "Women and Occupational Prestige: A Case of Vacuous Sex Equality." Signs 5:252-65.

England, Paula, and Stephen McLaughlin. 1979. "Sex Segregation of Jobs and Male-Female Income Differentials." In Discrimination in Organizations, edited by Rudolfo Alvarez, Kenneth G. Lutterman and Associates, pp. 189-213. San Francisco: Jossey-Bass.

Featherman, David, and Robert Hauser. 1976. "Sexual Inequalities and Socioeconomic Achievement in the U.S., 1962-73." American Sociological Review 41:462-83.

Ferree, Myra Marx. 1976. "Working-Class Jobs: Housework and Paid Work as Sources of Satisfaction." Social Problems 23:431-41.

Fidell, Linda S. 1970. "Empirical Verification of Sex Discrimination in Hiring Practices in Psychology." American Psychologist 25:1094-8.

Glazer, Nona. 1976. "Housework." Signs 1:905-22.

Glenn, N., A. Ross, and Judy C. Tully. 1974. "Patterns of Intergenerational Mobility of Females Through Marriage." American Sociological Review 39:683-99.

Goldthorpe, J. H., and Keith Hope. 1972. "Occupational Grading and Occupational Prestige." In The Analysis of Social Mobility: Methods and Approaches, edited by Keith Hope, pp. 19-79. London: Oxford University Press.

Havens, Elizabeth M., and Judy C. Tully. 1972. "Female Intergenerational Occupational Mobility: Comparisons of Patterns?" American Sociological Review 37:774-77.

Hicks, R. E. 1969. "The Relationship of Sex to Occupational Prestige in an African Country." Personnel and Guidance Journal 47:665-68.

Hodge, William, and Peter H. Rossi. 1978. "Intergroup Consensus in Occupational Prestige Ratings: A Case of Serendipity Lost and Regained." Socialwissenschaftliche Annalen 2:B59-73.

Hodge, William, Paul Siegel, and Peter H. Rossi. 1965. "Occupational Prestige in the United States: 1925-1963." American Journal of Sociology 20:286-302.

Jusenius, Carol L. 1975. "Occupational Change, 1967-71." In Dual Careers, edited by U.S. Department of Labor, Chapter 2. Washington, D.C.: U.S. Government Printing Office.

Kolstad, Andrew. 1977. "Sex Composition and the Social Standing of Occupations." Paper presented at the Annual Meeting of the American Sociological Association, Chicago, Illinois. Mimeographed.

Komarovsky, Mirra. 1962. Blue-Collar Marriage. New York: Random House.

Lopata, Helena Z. 1971. Occupation: Housewife. New York: Oxford University Press.

Marx, Karl. 1966. "A Note on Classes." In Class, Status and Power, second edition, edited by Seymour M. Lipset and Reinhard Bendix, pp. 5-6. New York: Free Press.

McClendon, McKee J. 1976. "The Occupational Status Attainment Processes of Males and Females." American Sociological Review 41:52-64.

McLaughlin, Steven D. 1978. "Occupational Sex Identification and the Assessment of Male and Female Earnings Inequality." American Sociological Review 43:909-21.

Menger, Clara. 1932. "The Social Status of Occupations for Women." Teachers College Record 33:696-704.

Nam, Charles B., and Mary G. Powers. 1983. The Socioeconomic Approach to Status Management. Houston: Cap and Gown Press.

Nam, Charles B., and Mary G. Powers. 1965. "Variations in Socioeconomic Structure by Race, Residence, and the Life Cycle." American Sociological Review 30:97-103.

National Longitudinal Surveys. Undated. "Attachment 4: Bose Index." In Codebook, compiled by Center for Human Resource Research, pp. 1-15. Worthington, Ohio: Center for Human Resource Research. Computer printout.

Nilson, Linda B. 1978. "The Social Standing of a Housewife." Journal of Marriage and the Family 40:541-48.

_____. 1976. "The Occupational and Sex Related Components of Social Standing." Sociology and Social Research 60:328-36.

Nock, Steven, and Peter H. Rossi. 1978. "Ascription Versus Achievement in the Attribution of Family Status." American Journal of Sociology 84:565-90.

Oakley, Ann. 1974. The Sociology of Housework. New York: Pantheon.

Oppenheimer, Valerie K. 1970. The Female Labor Force in the United States. Population Monograph Series no. 5. Berkeley: University of California.

Parcel, Toby L., and Charles W. Mueller. 1983. "Occupational Differentiation, Prestige, and Socioeconomic Status." Work and Occupations 10:49-80.

Parsons, Talcott. 1954. "A Revised Analytical Approach to Theory of Social Stratification." In Essays in Sociological Theory, revised edition, edited by Talcott Parsons, pp. 386-439. New York: Free Press.

Powell, Brian, and Jerry Jacobs. 1984. "Sex Differences in Occupational Prestige Rankings." Work and Occupations 11:283-308.

_____. 1983. "Sex and Consensus in Occupational Prestige Ratings." Sociology and Social Science Research 67:392-404.

Powers, Mary, and Joan Holmberg. 1982. "Occupational Status Scores: Changes Introduced by the Inclusion of Women." In Measures of Socioeconomic Status: Current Issues, edited by Mary Powers, pp. 55-81. Boulder: Westview Press.

Reiss, Albert J., Jr. 1961. Occupations and Social Status. New York: Free Press.

Ritter, Kathleen, and Lowell Hargens. 1975. "Occupational Positions and Class Identifications of Married Working Women: A Test of the Asymmetry Hypothesis." American Journal of Sociology 80:934-48.

Roper Organization. 1980. The 1980 Virginia Slims American Women's Opinion Poll. The Roper Organization.

Rossi, Peter H., and Steven S. Nock. 1982. Measuring Social Judgments: The Factorial Survey Approach. Beverly Hills: Sage.

Rossi, Peter H., William A. Sampson, Christine E. Bose, Guillermina Jasso, and Jeff Passel. 1974. "Measuring Household Social Standing." Social Science Research 3:169-90.

Sampson, William, and Peter H. Rossi. 1975. "Race and Family Standing." American Sociological Review 40:201-14.

Siegel, Paul. 1971. Prestige in the American Occupational Structure. Ph.D. Dissertation. University of Chicago, Chicago, Illinois.

Stefflre, Buford, Arthur Resnikoff, and Lawrence Lezotte. 1968. "The Relationship of Sex to Occupational Prestige." Personnel and Guidance Journal 46:765-72.

Stevens, Gillian, and David Featherman. 1981. "A Revised Socioeconomic Index of Occupational Status." Social Science Research 10:364-95.

Stevens, Raymond B. 1940. "The Attitudes of College Women Towards Women's Vocations." Journal of Applied Psychology 24:615-26.

Stevenson, Mary. 1975. "Relative Wages and Sex Segregation by Occupation." In Sex Discrimination and the Division of Labor, edited by Cynthia B. Lloyd, pp. 175-201. New York: Columbia University Press.

Strasser, Susan. 1982. Never Done. New York: Pantheon.

Treas, Judith, and Andrea Tyree. 1979. "Prestige Versus Socioeconomic Status in the Attainment Processes of American Men and Women." Social Science Research 8:201-21.

Treiman, Donald J. 1977. Occupational Prestige in Comparative Perspective. New York: Academic Press.

Treiman, Donald J., and Kermit Terrell. 1975. "Sex and the Process of Status Attainment: A Comparison of Working Women and Men." American Sociological Review 40:174-200.

Tyree, Andrea, and Judith Treas. 1974. "The Occupational and Marital Mobility of Women." American Sociological Review 39:293-307.

U.S. Bureau of the Census. 1984. 1980 Census of Population Subject Reports: Earnings by Occupation and Education. Report PC80-2-8B. Washington, D.C.: U.S. Government Printing Office.

_____. 1982. 1980 Census of Population: Alphabetical Index of Industries and Occupations. Final Edition PHC80-R3. Washington, D.C.: U.S. Government Printing Office.

_____. 1973. 1970 Census of Population Subject Reports: Occupational Characteristics. Final Report PC[2]-7A. Washington, D.C.: U.S. Government Printing Office.

_____. 1972. 1970 Census of Population: Occupation by Industry. Final Report PC[2]-70. Washington, D.C.: U.S. Government Printing Office.

_____. 1971. 1970 Census of Population: Alphabetical Index of Industries and Occupations. Washington, D.C.: U.S. Government Printing Office.

_____. 1963. 1960 Census of Population Subject Reports: Occupational Characteristics. Final Report PC[2]-7A. Washington, D.C.: U.S. Government Printing Office.

Vanek, Joann. 1978. "Household Technology and Social Status: Rising Living Standards, and Status and Residence Differences in Housework." Technology and Culture 19:361-75.

_____. 1976. "Job Satisfaction: The Case of Housework." Mimeographed.

_____. 1974. "Time Spent in Housework." Scientific American 231: 116-20.

Warner, W. Lloyd, M. Meeker, and K. Eells. 1949. Social Class in America. New York: Harper Torch Books.

Weber, Max. 1946. "Class, Status and Party." In From Max Weber: Essays in Sociology, edited by H. Gerth and C. Wright Mills, pp. 180-95. London: Oxford University Press.

INDEX

Acker, Joan R., 6
Arnott, C., 12

Bengtson, V., 12
Blau, Peter, 47, 58, 89
Blishen-Carroll Scores, 3, 14
Blishen-Roberts scores, 3, 14
Boyd and McRoberts, socioeconomic scores, 3
Bose, Christine E., 2, 6, 8, 12, 13
Bose Index: in gender segregated jobs, 67, 68, 69; in mixed incumbent scores, 64; male vs female incumbent, 66-69, 70; mode of analysis, 14, 26; scores, 26, 90, 97; NLS of 1960, 64, 65, 66, 70, 97; 1970, 65-66, 70; 1980, 64, 66-67, 70, 97 (see also Appendices C, D, E)
Bose Scores (see Bose Index)
Boyd, Monica, 3
Brawer, Melton J., 60

Census categories, 13, 14, 15, 16, 20, 26, 58
consensus: about nontraditional incumbents, 75, 77, 87; about occupations, 26, 31, 34, 72-73, 78, 79, 87-88, 93, 94-95; among individuals, 6, 13, 26, 72, 74, 75, 77, 78; on housewife's prestige, 45, 95 (see also variation)
control scores, 24, 32
Counts, George, 8

Davis, Kingsley, 5
DeJong, Peter Y., 4, 60
Dictionary of Occupational Titles (1965 edition), 13
dummy variable, 27, 28, 31, 32, 76

Duncan, Otis D., 47, 58, 89
Duncan socioeconomic status scores (SEI), 2, 3, 12, 14, 25, 26, 58, 59-64, 65, 89, 90, 96-97; compared with NORC, 60, 70 (see also Appendix C, SEI scores, Appendix E)
Dworkin, Rosalind, 12, 96

Education, 2, 3, 13, 25, 47; as a factor in prestige scores, 60-61, 62-68, 70, 71, 77 (see also prestige, Bose Index)
Ehrenreich, Barbara, 45
Eichler, Margaret, 12
England, Paula, 9, 37
English, Dierdre, 45
experimental treatments, 7, 18, 27-28, 53

Featherman, David, 2, 4, 61
female-dominated jobs, 3, 6, 8-9, 11, 15, 16, 31, 34, 35; definition of, 34; range of prestige scores in, 17, 34-35, 42, 49, 64, 93, 98 (see also stereotyped jobs)
Ferree, Myra Marx, 11
Fidell, Linda S., 17

Gender: explicit, 17-18, 27, 37, 41; implicit, 17, 27, 31, 33, 35, 37, 39 (see also percent female, stereotyped jobs); incumbent, 2, 3, 4, 5, 7, 8, 14, 16, 17, 27, 28, 31, 32-34, 35, 37, 41, 42 (see also prestige); respondent, 27, 28, 32; (see also incumbents, judgers, percent female, prestige scores, respondent characteristics, stereotyped jobs)

203

gender effects: 1960 census, 14; 1970 census, 14; 1980 census, 14 (see also prestige scores)
Glazer, Nona, 11
Glenn, N., 10

Hargens, Lowell, 1
Hauser, Robert, 4
Havens, Elizabeth M., 1
Hicks, R. E., 6-7
Hodge, William, 1, 19, 28, 89
Holmberg, Joan, 3
househusbands, 10, 25; prestige scores of, 45, 47, 51-55, 56, 96
housewives: blue collar, 51; full time, 11, 47; full time employed, 8, 11; income equivalents, 47, 48, 96; in NOINC treatment sample, 48; labor force equivalent, 45, 46, 47, 95; middle class, 11, 51; occupational ranking, 12; occupational role of, 10-11, 47; part time, 11; prestige scores, 12, 25, 45, 46, 47, 51, 53, 54, 56, 96; status of, 3, 4, 10-11, 12-13, 25, 44-46, 47, 49, 51, 56-57, 95-96; working class, 11-12 (see also prestige)

Income, 2, 3, 13, 25; differences, 9, 22-23, 42, 47; effect on prestige scores, 60-61, 62-68, 70, 71, 97 (see also Bose Index, prestige)
incumbent: female only, 2, 3, 7, 9, 12, 28, 31, 32, 37, 39, 53, 79; male, 2, 3, 7, 8, 32, 39; mixed, 4, 5, 7, 10, 41, 53, 54; nontraditional, 23, 35, 59, 68, 75, 77, 86, 87, 94; race, 19

Jacobs, Jerry, 6, 8, 72, 73, 79, 86, 94

judgers, 37-41
Jusenius, Carol L., 34

Kolstad, Andrew, 9, 13
Komarovsky, Mirra, 11, 49

Lopata, Helena, 10, 51

Male-dominated jobs, 3, 6, 15, 16, 34, 35; definition of, 34; range of prestige scores in, 17, 34, 35, 64 (see also stereotyped jobs)
married incumbents (see housewives, full time employed)
Marx, Karl, 15
McClendon, McKee, 4
McLaughlin, Steven, 9, 63
McRoberts, Hugh A., 3
Menger, Clara, 8, 12, 53, 96
mobility: career, 4, 56; female, 60; intergenerational, 4; occupational, 1, 2, 60; social, 4
Moore, Wilbert, 5
Mueller, Charles W., 2, 13

Nam and Powers Index, 2, 14, 61
Nam, Charles B., 60
National Longitudinal Surveys (NLS), 26, 64
Nilson, Linda B., 8, 12, 55
Nock, Steven, 1, 25
NOINC Scores, 24, 25, 27, 31, 32, 37, 42, Appendix C; compared with NORC Scores, 58-59; compared with SEI scores, 60-64
No-Incumbent treatment (NOINC), 8, 28, 31; effect on prestige scores, 32, 33, 34-35, 37, 41, 45, 47, 48, 58, 92, Appendix C
NORC prestige scale, 3, 17, 19, 20, 23, 24, 25, 31, 32, 34, 42, 58-59, 91; compared with NOINC, 58-59, 70

INDEX

Oakley, Ann, 11, 51
occupational categories, 2, 3, 6, 15, 16 (see also census categories)
occupational characteristics, 4, 5, 13, 14
occupational hierarchy (see occupational categories, occupational characteristics)
occupational prestige (see prestige)
occupational status, 1-3, 17, 89 (see also social standing)
Oppenheimer, Valerie K., 34

Parcel, Toby L., 2, 13
Parsons, Talcott, 5
Pearson Correlation Coefficient, 73
percent female, 13, 27, 31, 32, 33; effect on prestige score, 37, 42, 97; in occupational categories, 6, 15, 16, 17, 31, 32, 34, 35; in the total work force, 35 (see also total labor force
Powell, Brian, 6, 8, 72, 73, 79, 86, 94
Powers, Mary, 2, 3, 61
prestige, 4, 5; and class, 31; and race, 19; education and, 2, 3, 13, 25, 61; gendered, 3, 4, 5, 9, 99; homemaker, 11, 12; income and, 2, 3, 13, 25, 61; mixed incumbent, 63, 64; no incumbent, 62; occupational, 1-2, 3-5, 9-10, 13-14, 17, 18, 26, 32, 33, 41, 88, 90, 93 (see also education, income)
prestige scores, 14, 17, 24, 25, 27, 31, 91; as measurement of status, 1-3, 5, 14, 89-90; average, 17, 35, 37; effects of occupational characteristics, 31; gender effects, 31, 32; [prestige] incumbent gender effects, 31, 32, 35, 37, 39, 41, 42, 62, 63, 69, 79, 90; effects of respondent characteristics, 32, 33-34; male bias in, 32, 60, 61, 69, 96; mean prestige scores, 17, 35, 59, 79; Zambian sample, 7-8 (see also Blishen-Carroll, Blishen-Roberts, Bose Index, Boyd and McRoberts scores, Nam and Powers index, NOINC, NORC, Siegel Prestige Scale, Treiman International Prestige Scales, Appendices C and D)
prestige ratings (see prestige scores)

Questionnaires: analysis of, 23-24; college, 22-23; household, 22-23; in Bose study, 22, Appendix A

Rating task, 21-22, 91
Reiss, Albert, 12, 89
respondent characteristics, 2, 4, 14; age, 19, 20, 28, 33, 41, 54, 55, 94; education, 19, 20, 28, 33, 34, 41, 42, 54, 55; gender, 8, 9, 12, 18, 27, 32, 37-41, 42, 53-55; household status, 19-20, 21, 28, 33-34, 37, 39, 41, 54; income level, 19, 20; marital status, 54-55; race, 19, 33, 39; social standing, 9, 13, 28; (see also sample)
Ritter, Kathleen, 1
Robins, Stanley S., 60
Roper Organization, 28
Rossi, Peter H., 1, 19, 25, 28, 89, 96

Sample: college, 6, 7, 9, 20, 28, 31, 32, 33, 34, 41, 91; effect on prestige scores, 39,

[sample; effect on prestige scores] 41, 42, 56, 93, 94; household, 19-20, 28, 32, 33, 34, 37, 91; effect on prestige scores, 41, 42, 56, 93; occupational, 15, 16, Appendix B (see also respondent characteristics)
Sampson, William, 19
SEI scores (see Duncan socioeconomic scores)
sex inequality, 31, 39, 41
sexist ideology, 5
sex segregation, 16, 23, 34 (see also stereotyped jobs)
Siegel, Paul, 9, 20, 58, 59, 89
Siegel prestige scale, 15, 26, 58-59 (see also Appendix E)
social mobility, 4, 13, 14
social hierarchy: fairness of, 22, 31, 33
social standing, 1, 2, 4, 5, 14, 15; rating of, 21-22, 31 (see also prestige, NORC, SEI scores, Bose Index)
Stefflre, Buford, 6-7
stereotyped jobs, 2, 3-4, 6-7, 8, 23, 34-37, 42, 92, 94, 98

Stevens and Featherman, socioeconomic scores, 61
Stevens, Gillian, 3, 61
Stevens, Raymond B., 9
Stevenson, Mary, 9

Terrell, Kermit, 4, 9
Treas, Judith, 2
Treiman, Donald J., 4, 9
Treiman International Prestige Scale, 2
total labor force, 3, 14, 16 (see also percent female)
treatment effects, 32
Tully, Judy C., 1
Tyree, Andrea, 2

Vanek, Joann, 11, 47
variance analysis, 7, 64
variation: between samples, 34, 51-53, 73-77; in selected respondent characteristics, 76, 77, 78; occupational, 33, 37, 45-46; with incumbent treatment, 73

Warner, W. Lloyd, 5
Weber, Max, 5
women's movement, 1, 90, 92

ABOUT THE AUTHOR

CHRISTINE E. BOSE is an assistant professor of sociology at the State University of New York at Albany, where she also served as director of the Women's Studies Program from 1978 through 1981. Prior to that she was a member of the sociology faculty at the University of Washington.

Dr. Bose has published in the areas of occupational prestige, gender and status attainment, women's home and paid employment at the turn of the century, and the social impact of household technology. Her articles have appeared in American Sociological Review, Social Science Research, American Journal of Sociology, Women's Studies International Quarterly, and Technology and Culture. She is a founder of the interdisciplinary Women and Work Research Group, formed under a grant from the American Sociological Association Problems in the Discipline Program, which is developing an analysis of the hidden aspects of women's employment.

Dr. Bose holds a bachelor's degree in mathematics from Wagner College and a doctorate in sociology from The Johns Hopkins University.